GLASGOW, THE CLYDE AND SLAVERY

Stenlake Publishing Ltd.

© Stenlake Publishing Ltd, 2023.
Text compiled by D. Pettigrew
First published in the United Kingdom, 2023,
by Stenlake Publishing Ltd.
54-58 Mill Square,
Catrine, KA5 6RD

01290 551122
www.stenlake.co.uk

Printed by Claro Print Ltd.
Offices 26/27, 1 Spiersbridge Way,
Glasgow, G46 8NG

ISBN 978-1-84033-960-4

The publishers regret that they cannot supply copies of any pictures featured in this book.

Front cover: (upper) Germiston House, see page 30; (lower) Scotstoun House, see page 59.

Contents

Introduction 5

The City of Glasgow and Bearsden, Bishopbriggs, ... 13
Cambuslang, Clarkston, Milngavie,
Newton Mearns and Rutherglen

The south bank of the Clyde estuary: 83
Inverclyde and Renfrewshire including Neilston

The north bank of the Clyde estuary: 111
Clydebank to Dunoon

The Broomielaw in the early 1820s, drawn by John Fleming. On the left is Clyde Street looking towards the Bridgegate; on the right Carlton Place with Gorbals Parish Church, finished 1810 and demolished 1975. The Broomielaw Bridge (1772), in the foreground, was replaced in 1836 by the present Glasgow Bridge. In the distance is the Old Bridge built in 1345, demolished in 1850 and replaced by the Victoria Bridge of 1854.

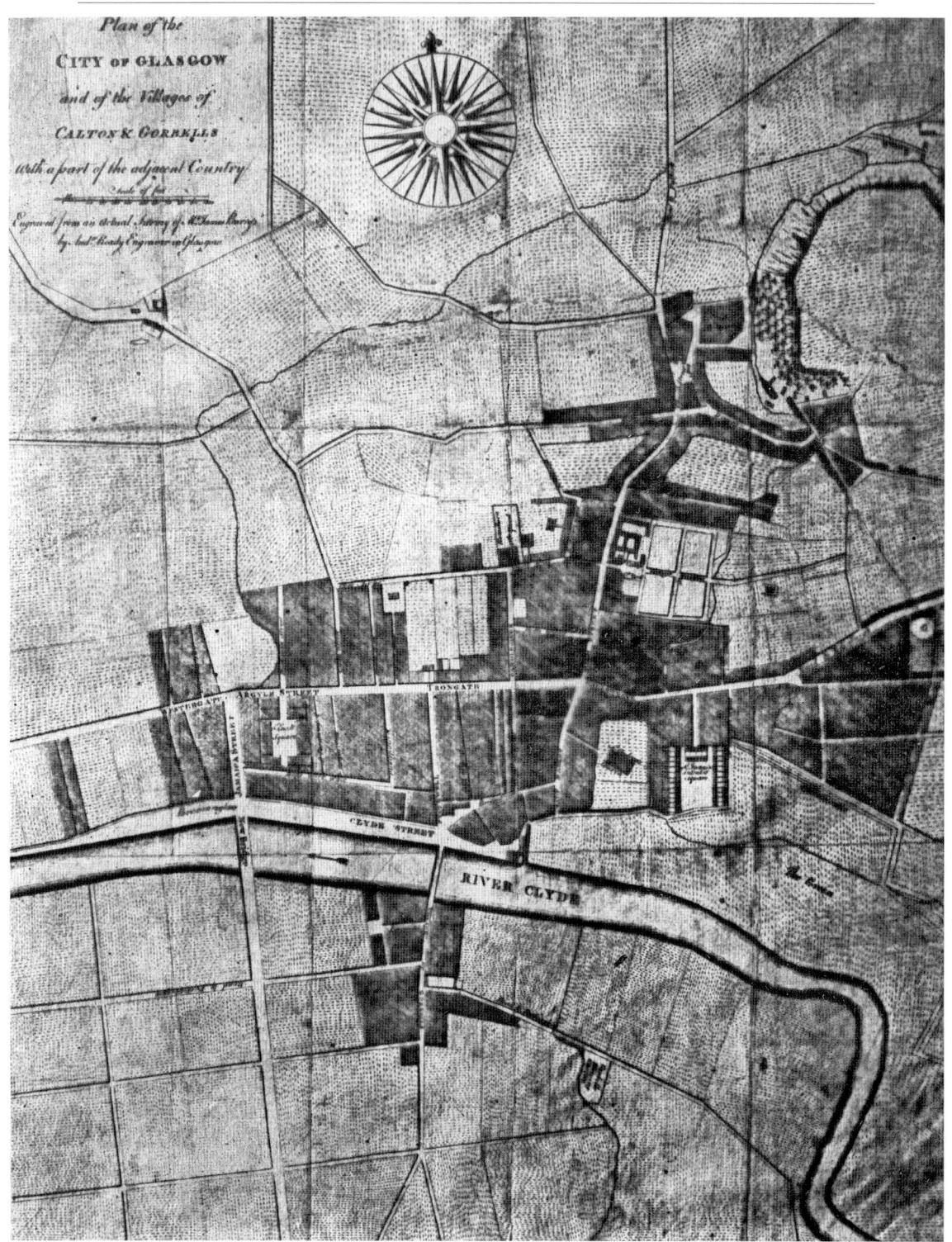
Glasgow in 1776.

INTRODUCTION

From the mid-sixteenth century until the 1830s, the British economy profited directly and significantly from the trade in enslaved people and from the industries that relied on their enforced labour. This trade received Royal endorsement from a charter of Charles II in 1663 and was not abolished until the passing of the Slave Trade Act in 1807. However, the Act only prohibited the buying and selling of people as slaves. Legal use of enslaved labourers continued for another 26 years until the Slavery Abolition Act of 1833, which came into force on 1 August 1834. Even then, enforced labour continued for any former slaves over the age of six, who became 'apprentices' and were made to work for minimal wages, if any, until this scheme ended in 1840. And none of these conditions applied to areas of the British Empire overseen by the East India Company, including India, Ceylon (Sri Lanka) and St Helena, where slavery continued until 1843.

Portugal, Spain, France, Denmark, Sweden, the Netherlands and Britain were the main slave trading nations of Europe. The slave trade developed as a 'triangular trade' whereby European ships took mixed goods, such as cloth, firearms, gunpowder, beads, alcohol, glassware, ceramics, metals and metalware[1], to the West African coast where they would be traded for African people who had already been captured for the purpose of exchange for these goods. These people were then forced onto ships – often after being held in slave 'forts' or 'stations' – and taken across the Atlantic on the 'middle passage', a journey of six to eight weeks. They were then sold into slavery in colonies in North and South America and the Caribbean. The ships would return to Europe carrying the commodities of these colonies – including tobacco, cotton, sugar, coffee, rice, rum and mahogany – produced using the enforced labour of people already enslaved there.

With colonies in North America, the Caribbean and South America, Britain had become the foremost slave-trading nation in the world by the 1730s.[2] Throughout the period of the slave trade, around 3.1 million African people were transported across the Atlantic by British ships, with only 2.7 million arriving alive.[3] These ships mostly left from the English ports of Bristol, Liverpool and London, though 27 slave ship journeys departed from the Scottish ports of Montrose, Leith, Port Glasgow and Greenock between 1706 and 1766, transporting around 5,000 people into slavery.[4]

Despite the relatively low numbers of slave voyages leaving from Scottish ports, Scots were involved in the slave trade in myriad ways: as sailors and captains on the slave ships, as doctors at the slave stations in Africa, as slave auctioneers, and as factors and business investors facilitating the trade. For example, the Scottish merchants Richard Oswald and Alexander Grant were owners of the slave-trading station of Bunce Island on the Sierra Leone River from 1748 to 1785. Here, people who had been kidnapped inland were incarcerated before transportation into slavery in the colonies. Many were farmers skilled in rice-growing who would fetch high prices in the rice-growing areas of Georgia and South Carolina. To facilitate this trade, Oswald developed strong business connections with the South Carolina rice planter Henry Laurens[5], one of many examples of the Scottish entrepreneurship that would make fortunes from the slavery-based economy. It was in this economy, rather than in the transportation of enslaved people, that Scots were most deeply and directly involved.

The Union of the Scottish and English Parliaments in 1707 gave Scottish merchants access to colonial markets. From that point on their presence in the Caribbean and in America grew significantly. Demand for American tobacco in Britain and Europe was enormous and Glasgow's geographical position facing the Atlantic put it in a prime position to take advantage. The city's tobacco trade developed from around 1740 and was given a major boost when the French government awarded it a monopoly of supply to the French market in 1747.[6] Glasgow became the international hub of this trade and the merchants and entrepreneurs involved in it became fantastically wealthy. These were the so-called 'tobacco lords', among them figures such as John Glassford, Andrew Buchanan, Archibald Ingram, Alexander Speirs and James Dunlop – all names that still feature in the topography of Glasgow.

The tobacco boom lasted until the outbreak of the American Revolutionary War in 1775 and some businesses, such as John Glassford's, failed as a result. However, while tobacco had been the main driver of economic success in the mid to late eighteenth century, the trade in Caribbean sugar had also been developing from the late 1600s and provided opportunities that attracted many young Scottish men looking to make fortunes, or at least a living, particularly after 1745. Famously, the draw of the Caribbean to Scots is symbolised by Robert Burns considering the option of taking employment on a Jamaican plantation. He didn't go through with this, but possibly as many as 20,000 Scots went to Britain's Caribbean colonies in the years up to 1800.[7] There they became involved at all levels of the plantation economy, which was principally fuelled by the demand for sugar.

Back in Scotland, as had happened with tobacco, businessmen made vast profits from sugar, many as owners of plantations; some became among the richest people in Britain. The 'tobacco lords' were replaced by the 'sugar barons' – men such as James Ewing, Robert Bogle and John Campbell. Some of them had spent years in the colonies and had seen the brutal conditions of chattel slavery first-hand – a profoundly violent system, built on acute human suffering, where the life expectancy of an adult African person forced into slavery could be as short as four years.[8] Those who were absentee landlords would not have witnessed this. But whatever their knowledge or experience of slavery, the priority was to protect and perpetuate their business interests – as attested by the existence of the Glasgow West India Association which served to maintain and advance the interests of Caribbean merchants and met in the Cunninghame Mansion, now the Glasgow Gallery of Modern Art. They continued to profit from a trade that depended on slave labour until the abolition of slavery in most British colonies in the 1830s. Even then, enormous sums of money were still to be made in the form of the compensation from the British government for the loss of their enslaved labourers.

Opposition to slavery had grown in British society throughout the eighteenth century and by the 1830s this opposition – combined with the waning economic importance of the slavery-based economy in the face of competition from other plantation economies outside the British Empire such as in Brazil, and the growing prevalence of uprisings of enslaved people[9] – meant that the argument for abolition was overwhelming. However, a powerful 'West India interest' of around 80 MPs connected to Caribbean slavery, and other MPs who supported them, campaigned for both compensation for slave owners and for the introduction of the period of 'apprenticeship' to cushion the financial blow before the final end to enforced labour.

To pass the Slavery Abolition Act of 1833, the British Government agreed to £20 million for this compensation, equivalent to around 40% of its annual expenditure. The figure (which Bank of England research estimated to be the equivalent of £1,958 million in 2022[10]) was finally paid off by the British taxpayer in 2015, though it should be noted that the 182-year payment term was more an aspect of the method of payment, rather than the size of the borrowing.[11]

The sum was raised through a public loan from city financiers and from government stocks. Certificates of compensation were given to slave owners and their cash was literally collected at the Cashier's Office of the Bank of England, though usually by agents representing the slave owners,[12] who received a share of the compensation as commission for their services. No compensation was ever paid by the British state to any enslaved people, nor any apology made.[13/14]

Glasgow, Greenock and Port Glasgow's connections to the tobacco and sugar trades have always been widely known and - as this book shows – the people involved have been celebrated in various ways, often in the naming of streets. These connections have always been controversial too, though in recent years there has been a wider re-evaluation of the legacy they have created.

In the area of academic historical research, serious examination of Scotland's links to the slavery-based economy has been ongoing for decades, uncovering the depth of Scots' involvement. Recently, organisations such as local authorities and universities have assessed their connections to historic slavery. Some information in this book draws on reports commissioned by Glasgow City Council and Inverclyde Council to examine their communities' links to slavery, and since 2019 the University of Glasgow has made initiatives to address its own historical links to the slavery-based economy. Descendants of Scottish landowners who profited from it, including the Gladstone family, are also working to raise awareness and acknowledge the legacy of slavery in Britain.[15]

The true extent of Scotland's involvement in slavery has also become clearer since 2013 when University College London opened its database of around 46,000 claims for compensation for the loss of enslaved labour that the British Government received after the passing of the Slavery Abolition Act of 1833.[16] The database reveals the names of thousands of British people who owned enslaved people at that time and who owed most of their wealth to their labour. Proportionally, a higher number of claims were awarded to Scots than to people of any other part of the United Kingdom. Some claims amounted to the equal of millions of pounds today, meaning that the descendants of those involved in slavery continued to benefit from its proceeds for decades to come. On a broader level, many of those who profited from slavery were businessmen who invested their profits in grand country estates and townhouses – a number of which are illustrated here – as well as in industry, churches, railways, educational and other institutions. The accumulated legacy of this spending is still being quantified by historians, but it made a significant contribution to British society. In Glasgow, institutions such as the City Council, the Mitchell Library and the University of Glasgow benefitted from bequests made by businessmen of the slavery-based economy.

This book offers an overview of locations in Glasgow and its surrounding areas that are connected to slavery and the slavery-based economy of the eighteenth and nineteenth centuries. In doing so it seeks to illustrate the part slavery played in shaping the region and how the involvement of past generations lingers with us today.

The amounts shown as being awarded by the Slave Compensation Commission were massive. One thousand pounds awarded in 1835 is roughly equivalent to a relative income value of £1.3 million in 2023. The website www.measuringworth.com is a useful tool for making comparisons.

Map produced in 1807 by Peter Fleming.

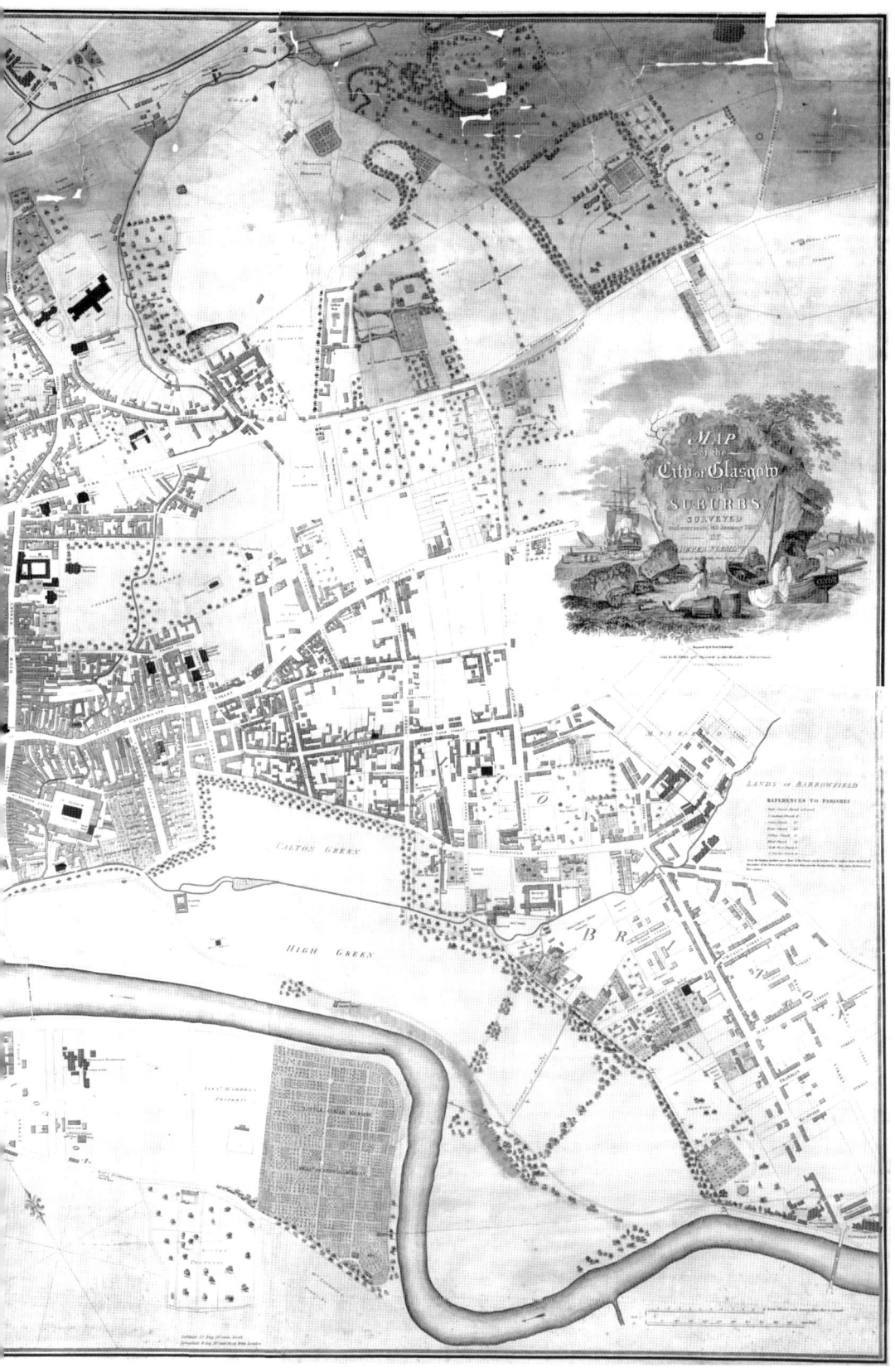

Reproduced with the permission of the National Library of Scotland. This image is licensed under the Creative Commons (CC-BY) licence. To view the licence visit https://creativecommons.org/licenses/by/4.0/

Further Reading

Much of the information in this book draws from recent research by Scottish historians, including Stephen Mullen, Stuart Nisbet and David Alston. This book offers an overview: those who want to know more are urged to investigate the sources listed below, all of them freely available online.

Canmore: National Record of the Historic Environment, Historic Environment Scotland.
  Weblink: https://canmore.org.uk
  Appears as *Canmore* in references.

Glasgow, Slavery and Atlantic Commerce: An Audit of Historical Connections and Modern Legacies: Report for Glasgow City Council, March 2022, by Stephen Mullen.
  Weblink: https://www.glasgow.gov.uk/CHttpHandler.ashx?id=56499&p=0
  Appears as *Glasgow, Slavery and Atlantic Commerce* in references.

Inverclyde's Historical Links to Slavery – Final Report, 25 January 2022, Inverclyde Council: Corporate Director Education, Communities and Organisational Development (Alana Ward, Service Manager).
  Weblink: https://www.inverclyde.gov.uk/meetings/documents/14912/05%20inverclyde's%20historical%20links%20to%20slavery%20report.pdf
  Appears as *Inverclyde* in references.

It Wisnae Us – The Truth about Glasgow and Slavery, 2023: Text by Stephen Mullen, website design by Jon Jardine.
  Weblink: https://it.wisnae.us/
  Appears as *It Wisnae Us* in references.

Legacies of British Slavery database: Centre for the Study of the Legacies of British Slavery, University College London.
  Weblink: https://www.ucl.ac.uk/lbs/
  Appears as *LBS database* in references.

Legacies of Slavery in Glasgow Museums and Collections: Glasgow Museums.
  Weblink: https://glasgowmuseumsslavery.co.uk/
  Appears as *Legacies of Slavery* in references.

TheGlasgowStory, 2004, University of Glasgow / University of Strathclyde / Glasgow City Council / New Opportunities Fund / Scottish Enterprise Glasgow.
  Weblink: https://www.theglasgowstory.com
  Appears as *TheGlasgowStory* in references.

The Old Country Houses of the Old Glasgow Gentry (2nd edition, 1878): John Guthrie Smith and John Oswald Mitchell.
  Weblink: http://www.glasgowwestaddress.co.uk/Old_Country_Houses/Contents.htm
  Appears as *Old Country Houses* in references.

References

1. Stanley B. Alpert, 'What Africans Got for Their Slaves: A Master List of European Trade Goods', *History in Africa*, vol. 22, 1995, pp. 5–43. JSTOR: https://doi.org/10.2307/3171906.
2. 'The Transatlantic Slave Trade', 2021, *Heritage Collections UK Parliament:* https://heritagecollections.parliament.uk/stories/the-transatlantic-slave-trade/
3. 'Slavery and the British transatlantic slave trade', *The National Archives*: https://www.nationalarchives.gov.uk/help-with-your-research/research-guides/british-transatlantic-slave-trade-records/
4. 'Scots Involvement in the Atlantic Slave Trade', *National Library of Scotland*: https://www.nls.uk/collections/scotland-and-the-slave-trade/involvement/
5. 'Bunce Island History', 2023, *Yale MacMillan Centre, Yale University*: https://glc.yale.edu/lectures/evening-lectures/past-lectures/20042005/bunce-island/bunce-island-history
6. 'The Industrial Revolution (II), 19.9.2014, *BBC: The Enlightenment and Industrial Revolution*: https://www.bbc.co.uk/history/scottishhistory/enlightenment/features_enlightenment_industy2.shtml
7. 'Sugar and Slavery', *It Wisnae Us*: https://it.wisnae.us/sugar-and-slavery/
8. 'My ancestors profited from slavery. Here's how I am starting to atone for that', Alex Renton, 24.4.2023, *The Guardian*: https://www.theguardian.com/commentisfree/2023/apr/24/ancestors-profit-slavery-atone-enslaved-people
9. Natasha L. Henry, 'Slavery Abolition Act United Kingdon [1833]', *Britannica*: https://www.britannica.com/topic/Slavery-Abolition-Act
10. Michael Anson and Michael D. Bennett, 'The collection of slavery compensation, 1835-43', Staff Working Paper No. 1,006, November 2022, p. 1, *Bank of England*: https://www.bankofengland.co.uk/-/media/boe/files/working-paper/2022/the-collection-of-slavery-compensation-1835-43.pdf
11. HM Treasury, 'Freedom of Information Act 2000: Slavery Abolition Act 1833', 31.1.2018: https://assets.publishing.service.gov.uk/government/uploads/system/uploads/attachment_data/file/680456/FOI2018-00186_-_Slavery_Abolition_Act_1833_-_pdf_for_disclosure_log__003_.pdf
12. Michael Anson and Michael D. Bennett, 'The collection of slavery compensation, 1835-43', Staff Working Paper No. 1,006, November 2022, p. 1, *Bank of England*: https://www.bankofengland.co.uk/-/media/boe/files/working-paper/2022/the-collection-of-slavery-compensation-1835-43.pdf
13. Kris Manjapra, 'When Will Britain Face Up to its Crimes Against Humanity?', 29.3.2018, *The Guardian*: https://www.theguardian.com/news/2018/mar/29/slavery-abolition-compensation-when-will-britain-face-up-to-its-crimes-against-humanity
14. Aletha Adu, 'Rishi Sunak refuses to apologise for UK slave trade or to pledge reparations', 26.4.2023, *The Guardian*: https://www.theguardian.com/world/2023/apr/26/rishi-sunak-refuses-to-apologise-for-uk-slave-trade-or-to-pledge-reparations
15. Heirs of Slavery: https://www.heirsofslavery.org/
16. Naomi Fowler, Britain's Slave Owner Compensation Loan, reparations and tax havenry', 9.6.2020, *Tax Justice Network*: https://taxjustice.net/2020/06/09/slavery-compensation-uk-questions/

The Tontine Hotel in Trongate 1820s, drawn by J. Knox. The Town Hall attached to the Tolbooth steeple contained the assembly rooms and the piazza outside was used by the tobacco lords to discuss business.

The Buckshead Hotel in Argyle Street, painted by Thomas Fairbairn 1849.

The City of Glasgow
and Bearsden, Bishopbriggs,
Cambuslang, Clarkston, Milngavie,
Newton Mearns and Rutherglen

Abercromby Street

Named after Menstrie-born Lieutenant General Sir Ralph Abercromby (1734-1801), Commander of the Leeward and Windward Islands and Governor of Trinidad. In 1796/97[17], his armies – which used as soldiers enslaved people from Africa[18] – captured the islands of St Lucia, St Vincent, Grenada, Trinidad and Tobago, and the region of Demerara in the Guineans (now Guyana), placing them under British control.

Allison Street

Sir Archibald Alison (1792-1867) was a sheriff of Lanarkshire[19] and Rector of both Glasgow University and Aberdeen University. Along with his brother, William Pulteney Alison (1790-1859), a professor of medicine and medical theory at Edinburgh University, and Alexander Cruikshank of Stracathro House, Angus, he was a trustee of Bellevue estate, Jamaica. (This was owned by a brother-in-law of the Alisons, Colonel John Gerard, who had died in 1824[20].) Together they were awarded over £4,081 from the Slave Compensation Commission for the 152 people enslaved on the estate. Archibald Alison was a pro-slavery defender of the Confederate states during the American Civil War.[21] After moving to Glasgow in 1835, he lived in Possil House until his death.

Allison Street was laid out in in the late 1860s, around the time of Sir Archibald Alison's death so it could have been named to commemorate him. However, the spelling contains an extra 'l' and it crosses Daisy and Annette Streets, named after William S. Dixon of Govanhill's daughters, so perhaps it is named after another woman.

Argyle Street

Site of three townhouses belonging to merchants in Virginia tobacco. Colin Dunlop built his mansion at the junction of Argyle Street and Dunlop Street in 1751. Around the same period another tobacco merchant, John Murdoch[22], built an even larger mansion adjacent. This became the Buck's Head Hotel in 1790[23] and was pulled down and replaced by the existing Buck's Head Warehouse, designed by Alexander 'Greek' Thomson, in 1862.[24] Dunlop's mansion, which latterly housed shop premises, lasted until 1922.[25] Both Dunlop and Murdoch served as Lord Provosts. Murdoch's country home was Rosebank in Cambuslang. The third mansion was The Black House[26], so called for the colour of stone it was built from, which was erected at the corner of Argyle Street (West Gait) and Queen Street (Cow Loan) either in 1753 or 1776; at the latter date it was certainly in the ownership of tobacco merchant John McCall. After his death in 1790, the house was sold and a tenement was built on its site.[27]

Balshagray Avenue / Balshagray Drive
The lands of Balshagray were bought in 1759 by the Caribbean merchants, brothers Richard and Alexander Oswald of Scotstoun.[28]

Bellahouston House.

Bellahouston Park

James Rowan (b. 1691) bought the estate of Bellahouston in 1726.[29] Known as 'James Rowan of Maryland', the purchase was presumably made on his return from a career as a tobacco trader.[30] In 1824 the estate passed to Moses Steven of Polmadie (1748-1831), partner in Caribbean merchant firm Buchanan, Steven & Co.[31] His co-partners in the firm were James Buchanan of Dowanhill and James Dennistoun of Golfhill. He also bought Dumbreck House, joining the two estates and renaming the house as Bellahouston House. Glasgow Corporation acquired the estate in 1892[32] and the park opened to the public in 1896.

Belvidere Avenue / Belvidere Gate / Belvidere Terrace / Belvidere Hospital

These streets were named after Belvidere House, built in 1760 by tobacco merchant, industrialist and banker John McCall[33] (1715-90) on land in the Parkhead area between

Belvidere House.

London Road and the River Clyde. McCall also lived at the city centre mansion The Black House, where his neighbours included other tobacco lords such as his business partner John Glassford.[34] McCall died at Belvidere in 1790 and the house was bought by his son-in-law, Robert McNair, grandson of the Robert McNair (d. 1779) who started the Easter Sugar House on Gallowgate in the mid 1700s, a business dependent on Caribbean trade. According to Smith and Mitchell, this business eventually passed to grandson Robert, in partnership with his brother James McNair of Calder Park, and they moved it to purpose-built premises – 'a huge clumsy looking edifice of four storeys' – at the corner of Ingram and Queen Streets, opposite the Cunninghame mansion.[35] McNair of Belvidere sold the house to Mungo Nutter Campbell (1785-1862), a Caribbean merchant who was Lord Provost from 1824 to 1826. He was partner in the firm John Campbell Senior & Co.[36] Between 1835 and 1837 he shared in compensation awards of over £77,188 for ten plantations in Grenada, Guyana and St Vincent. At the time of abolition, these enslaved a total of 1,609 people.[37] His country residence was Ballimore House by Loch Fyne, Argyll. The city council took ownership of Belvidere in 1870 and demolished it, then built the hospital on London Road which was demolished in 1999.[38] Houses now occupy the site.

Blawarthill

East of Garscadden, the name of this eighteenth-century estate lives on in Blawarthill Parish Church.[39] The estate's owners included the tobacco lords George Oswald and Alexander Speirs.[40]

Blythswood Place, at the junction of St Vincent and Wellington Streets, in the late 1820s, drawn by John Fleming.

Blythswood Square / Blythswood Place

The Blythswood estate once stretched from Glasgow to Renfrew and was owned in the 1820s by Glasgow MP Archibald Campbell (c. 1763-1838), who represented the interests of Glasgow Caribbean merchants in Parliament. Mungo Nutter Campbell, Caribbean merchant and a Lord Provost, had his city address at '5 Blythswood Place' in 1826. It was around this time that Archibald Campbell began to feu parts of this area for house building.[41]

Bridgegate

The Merchants House was established in 1601 with its first hall or 'hospital' in the Bridgegate; it was rebuilt in 1659 and its steeple was added in 1665.[42] The latter was later incorporated into the Glasgow fish market[43], which is now The Briggait, a complex of offices, artists' studios and exhibition spaces. At the time of the transatlantic slavery-based economy, The Merchants House was an influential merchants' organisation, with many members – a number of whom were involved with Virginia and Caribbean trade – becoming city councillors and Lord Provosts.[44] Some of its members left bequests for charitable funds which came from profits made in the slavery-based economy. The Merchants House is now a registered charity based in grand 1874 premises on George Square, opposite the City Chambers. It has acknowledged and addressed its links to the slavery-based economy[45] of the eighteenth and nineteenth centuries.

Bridgegate from the west, c. 1828, drawn by John Fleming.

The manager's house at the Delftfield Pottery, painted by William Simpson in 1848. The buildings of the works are in the background. The line of the modern James Watt Street runs between those buildings and the manager's house along what was Delfthouse Lane. James Watt was an investor and adviser to the company and is said to have lodged in the house in the 1760s. A few years earlier the notorious Elspeth Simpson was a servant there. She married Robert Buchan, a worker at the pottery. Shortly afterwards she began having religious hallucinations and would later declare herself a prophet and form a sect known as the Buchanites.

Brown Street

Site of the Delftfield Pottery, which was established in 1748 and is an example of the diverse business interests of tobacco lords as it was set up by Lawrence and Robert Dinwiddie of Germiston. Robert was Governor of Virginia (and owned slaves) so the pottery's earthenware and creamware products were exported to America. Lawrence was a tobacco merchant and also a partner in the Port Glasgow Rope and Duck Company. Later, James Watt became a partner in the business and his son eventually took it over until it stopped production in 1812.[46] A tobacco warehouse was built on the site in 1854.[47] Its frontage is on James Watt Street, which runs parallel to Brown Street, and this is still in use as storage units.

Buchanan Street

Andrew Buchanan (1725-83), co-partner in the Virginia tobacco firms Andrew Buchanan & Co. and Buchanan, Hastie & Co.[48], bought land to build a home in central

Glasgow in 1763. While other business interests continued, these firms folded in the 1770s, partly due to the loss of estates in the American Revolutionary War, and the land was feued out for house building thereafter. Buchanan was a nephew of tobacco lord Andrew Buchanan of Drumpellier, Lanarkshire (1690-1759).

Calderpark Road / Calderpark Gardens

In the vicinity of these streets stood the mansion and estate of Calder Park[49], which was built by sugar refiner James McNair around 1800.[50] With his brother Robert, he co-owned a sugar refinery on Ingram Street.

Calder Park House.

Camphill House

Now flats, this house in Queen's Park was built in the early 1800s as the home of Robert Thomson Junior (1771-81), partner in the cotton manufacturing firm Robert Thomson & Sons which was established by his father. The firm is very likely to have used cotton from Caribbean plantations.[51] Its factory was the Adelphi Mill in Hutchesontown; this was succeeded by the New Adephi Mill, part of which still survives as offices at 203 Rutherglen Road.[52]

Candleriggs

Site of Wester Sugar Works, established in 1667 to process Caribbean sugar. Other Glasgow sugar works were at Gallowgate, King Street and Stockwell Street and Smith and Mitchell recorded that the McNair family had one on Ingram Street.[53] John Stark, Lord Provost in 1725/26, was a partner[54], as was Caribbean merchant James Coulter[55] (d. 1788), who was also a partner in the King Street Sugar Works.

Cardross Street

Cardross Street was named after the town where the Dennistoun family had their estate, Colgrain[56], and seat, Camis Eskan House. They were Caribbean sugar importers.

Carmyle

The Dunlop family enjoyed 'superiority'[57] over the lands of Carmyle and after the 1793 failure of the Virginia tobacco business – started by Colin Dunlop – Colin's son James started coal mining in the area, maintaining the family wealth.

Cathedral Square / Cathedral Precinct

The site of two statues commemorating men linked to the slave trade, though in opposing ways. The equestrian statue of King William III (1650-1702) commemorates the monarch who was a shareholder and governor of the Royal African Company, which had been set up by the Stuart royal family to exploit gold fields that had been found in Gambia and then developed a trade in enslaved people with Caribbean plantations. Between 1672 and 1731 the company transported 187,679 people across the Atlantic, of whom 39,497 died en route.[58] William received a large proportion of his shares from the notorious slave trader Edward Colston of Bristol.[59] The monument to David Livingstone (1813-73) commemorates the famous missionary who campaigned against the enslavement of African people by other groups in the years after the abolition of slavery in the British Empire.

King William III statue, Cathedral Square.

Craigton

Lying north-west of Bellahouston Park, this area of housing stands on what were once the lands of Craigton House and estate, purchased by the merchant John Ritchie in 1746. It later became the home of his son, James (1722-99), one of the most successful of the Glasgow tobacco lords trading in Virginia.[60] His son, Henry Ritchie[61] (d. 1843), sold the house in 1830, moving to Busbie House which was near Knockentiber, Ayrshire. In 1836/37 he shared in a compensation award of over £4,476 for the 214 enslaved people on two plantations in St Elizabeth Parish, Jamaica.

Craigton House.

Cochrane Street

Previously Cotton Street, this was renamed in 1799 after Andrew Cochrane (1693-1777), tobacco lord and partner in Virginia tobacco importers Cochrane, Murdoch & Co.[62] with his brother-in-law John Murdoch (1709-76). Both men served as Lord Provost three times. Cochrane was also connected to the King Street Sugar House. There is a monument to him in the nave of Glasgow Cathedral.

Colbert Street

This was one of several streets (see also *Franklin Street*) laid out by Henry Monteith, cotton manufacturer, to house workers at his nearby Barrowfield Dye Works in Dalmarnock. He named the streets after men he admired.[63] Jean-Baptiste Colbert was Minister of State for Louis XIV of France and was influential in the development of 'the Black Code' which laid down conditions for slavery in French colonies.[64]

Colgrain Terrace

This Springburn address, now gone (though the name lives on, along with Colgrain Avenue, in a new-build estate in Ruchill), was named after the Argyll family seat of the Dennistoun family.[65] This family was not related to the Dennistouns of Golfhill who helped to establish the suburb of Dennistoun.

Cowlairs

Between 1778 and 1813 this estate and mansion was in the ownership of the Scott family, firstly Robert Scott and then Allan Scott, partner in Caribbean merchants Bogle and Scott.[66] His son, Michael Scott (1789-1833), was born at the house. After graduating from Glasgow University, he worked in Jamaica for Robert Bogle of Gilmorehill between 1806 and 1822. His experiences in the Caribbean formed the basis of a novel called *Tom Crindle's Log* which was serialised in *Blackwood's Magazine*[67] and '... actively and persistently perpetuated the prejudice that blacks in the Caribbean were inferior.'[68] He is known to have sold enslaved people in Jamaica and was co-owner of many others, including up to 103 who were held at Stratton Hall estate, St Thomas-in-the-East Parish, of which he was joint owner.[69] In the latter half of the nineteenth century, the Cowlairs estate became the site of the largest railway works in Scotland.[70]

Cowlairs House.

Craigpark House.

Craigpark / Craigpark Drive

From 1798 the Craigpark estate was owned by James MacKenzie, a merchant who 'received his mercantile training in the counting house of John Glassford' and became Lord Provost in 1806. Mackenzie built Craigpark House. In 1850 the estate was sold to Alexander Dennistoun of Golfhill and the house was demolished as part of the development of Dennistoun.[71]

Cromwell Street

As Lord Protector of England, Oliver Cromwell (1599-1658) launched a policy of imperial expansion known as the 'Western Design'[72] which secured possession of Jamaica. Cromwell was earlier a proponent of transporting Irish people to Barbados, where it is likely some ended up in enslavement; he was personally involved in ordering this after the infamous Siege of Drogheda in 1649.[73]

Daldowie

In 1724 Daldowie estate came into the ownership of merchant Robert Bogle of Shettleston (1669-1734); his son, George Bogle (1700-84), went on to build Daldowie

Daldowie House.

House. George Bogle was a Rector of Glasgow University three times and was a Caribbean and Virginia trader in tobacco and sugar.[74] He was an associate of John Glassford and a member of the Tontine Society.[75] George's descendants went on to further the family's connections to the slavery-based economy, among them George Bogle of Rosemount, Symington, Ayrshire, Robert Bogle and Archibald Bogle of Gilmorehill, Glasgow, and Hugh Bogle of Calderbank, North Lanarkshire. Daldowie House was later demolished and Daldowie Crematorium was built on the site in 1955.[76]

Dennistoun

Alexander Dennistoun, whose family firm was involved in the slavery-based economy, founded this district.

Dinwiddie Street

This street in Germiston was named for the Dinwiddie family, Virginia tobacco traders, who owned the Germiston estate.

Dowanhill / Dowanhill Street / Dowanhill Place / Dowanhill Terrace

Dowanhill was once an estate that belonged to James Buchanan (1756-1844), partner in the Caribbean trading firms Buchanan, Steven & Co., Dennistoun, Buchanan & Co.[77] and also William Duff & Co. He was also a member of the Glasgow West India

Association which advanced the interests of Glasgow merchants involved in Caribbean trade.[78] The estate passed to James's son, John, who sold it in 1853. The next owner, Thomas Lucas Paterson, began developing it as a residential area.[79] Jefferson Davies, ex-President of the Confederate States of America, stayed in Dowanhill in 1869 while visiting James Smith.[80]

Dunlop Street

Colin Dunlop (1706-77) was a Glasgow tobacco lord who traded with Virginia. He was also a Lord Provost and a founder of the city's first bank, the Ship Bank.[81] From 1749[82] he lived in a townhouse which stood on Argyle Street, close to Dunlop Street. His firm, Colin Dunlop & Sons, was continued by his son James (b. 1742), though it failed after the loss of the Virginia trade due to the American Revolutionary War. However, James then concentrated on developing the coal mining that the family had already started in Carmyle in 1762.[83] He later bought Tollcross estate with the profits and the continuation of the family wealth was sustained by mining and iron working rather than involvement in the slavery-based economy.[84]

Easterhill Street / Easterhill Place

The Easterhill estate once took up part of Tollcross. From 1750 to 1783 it belonged to tobacco merchant Archibald Smellie, who built Easterhill House and also owned a coal mine in the area[85] (the house stood near the present Colliery Road, Street and Gate[86]). The American Revolutionary War affected his business to the point where he

Easterhill House.

had to sell Easterhill in 1783 to James Hopkirk, another Virginia merchant, though he in turn sold it, possibly for the same reason, to Robert Findlay, Virginia and Caribbean merchant, the following year. It remained in the Findlay family's possession until the 1930s.[87]

Elderslie Street

Named for the tobacco lord Alexander Speirs of Elderslie (1714-1782). Speirs Wharf is also named after him.

Fox Street

Charles James Fox (1749-1806) was a politician who became Britain's first Foreign Secretary and supported William Wilberforce's campaign to end the slave trade. In a 1789 parliamentary debate on the issue of government regulation of the slave trade, he took the position that 'he knew of no such thing as regulation of robbery or a restriction of murder. There was no medium; the legislature must either abolish the trade or avow their own criminality.'[88] In 1806 Parliament voted for his resolution that it abolish the slave trade and this led to the passing of the Slave Trade Act, banning the trade throughout much of the British Empire, in March 1807. Fox had died the previous September.[89]

Franklin Street

Laid out by Henry Monteith for workers at his dye works and named by him after American statesman Benjamin Franklin (1705-90), a signatory of the United States Declaration of Independence. Franklin is known to have had enslaved people in his household[90] though after the Declaration of Independence he became a supporter of the abolition of slavery and petitioned Congress to end the slave trade.[91]

Gallowgate

After Jamaica became a British possession in 1655, the sugar trade to Scotland began in earnest and required the labour of enslaved people to flourish. Slavery is commonly thought of as an eighteenth-century phenomenon but hundreds of thousands of African people were being trafficked to Carribean islands from the mid-seventeenth century[92] and Scotland, politically independent before the Act of Union in 1707, was profiting from this.[93] On the south side of Gallowgate was the Easter Sugar House, established in 1669.[94] This processed semi-refined muscavado into various sugar products, including spirits. An original partner was James Peadie, twice Lord Provost between 1691 and 1698.[95] Other sugar houses were at King Street, Stockwell Street and Candleriggs.

Gallowgate was the site of the Black Boy Tavern[96] (there was also a Black Boy Close in the vicinity[97]), most likely named after the city elite's taste for having enslaved

The Easter Sugar House in the Gallowgate, sketched c. 1845 by William Simpson.

African page boys in their service, one of whom is featured in a portrait of John Glassford and his family.[98]

No. 161 Gallowgate[99] was the home and grocery of William Smeal (1792-1877), a Quaker who was a founder with the Rev. Dr Ralph Wardlaw of the Glasgow Anti-Slavery Society. After the abolition of British slavery in 1833, this became the Glasgow Emancipation Society, focused on the abolition of slavery in the United States (there was also a Glasgow Ladies' Emancipation Society, formed by Smeal's sister Jane). Smeal invited the American anti-slavery campaigner Frederick Douglass to speak in Glasgow in 1846 and Douglass stayed at his home.

George Square / George Street

George Square and Street are so-named for King George III (1738-1820), monarch from 1760 and throughout the period that saw the highest British involvement with the transatlantic slave trade and Caribbean slavery. Privately, George owned no enslaved people himself and there is evidence from the 1750s, when he was a teenager, that he thought slavery to be 'repugnant'.[100] However, there is also evidence that as monarch he sought to preserve the Caribbean colonies (and his son, later William IV, was a prominent defender of slavery).[101] He signed the Slave Trade Act of 1807 into law. The area of Kingston in Glasgow is also named after him.[102]

George Square from the south-east. In 1828, when John Fleming drew this view, the only statue in the square was of Sir John Moore. In the north-west corner (left of centre) stands the West George Street Chapel, where Rev. Dr Ralph Wardlaw was pastor. None of these, the square's original buildings, have survived; the last, on the north-east corner (beyond the carriages), was demolished in 1973.

The 1874 building of The Merchants House faces onto the square. The square itself features a number of statues commemorating men who were involved in some way with slavery and the slavery-based economy. Both Glasgow-born, John Moore (1761-1809) and Colin Campbell (1792-1863) were officers of the British Army whose service defended the slavery system. Moore served under Sir Ralph Abercromby in his Caribbean campaign of the late 1700s and was Governor of St Lucia in 1796[103], while Campbell, as a young officer, was stationed in Barbados and Demerara (now part of Guyana), where he may have been involved in quelling a slave revolt and was a member of the court martial which sentenced the alleged instigator of the revolt – a British missionary – to death.[104]

Other relevant statues commemorate James Oswald (1779-1853) who was a Caribbean merchant and MP for Glasgow, the engineer James Watt (1736-1819) who is known to have trafficked an enslaved child, Prime Minister William Gladstone (1809-98) who was from a plantation-owning family, and Prime Minister Robert Peel Junior (1788-1850), whose family wealth was based on the cotton manufacturing business started by his father, who was also an MP and who actively campaigned against the abolition of slavery. As a politician Peel Junior defended the system of plantation slavery and promoted caution on the issue of abolition.[105] Both Gladstone and Peel served as Rectors of Glasgow University.

Statues of Sir John Moore (*left*) and Colin Campbell 1st Baron Clyde (*right*) in George Square. Behind them on the column is the statue of Sir Walter Scott.

Germiston House.

Germiston

The Germiston estate and house (built in 1690)[106] belonged to the Dinwiddie family. Robert Dinwiddie Senior was an investor in the tobacco industry and his son Lawrence (1697-1764) followed him into the business, becoming successful enough to be considered one of the tobacco lords. He owned his own tobacco-importing ships and his brother, Robert Dinwiddie (1693-1770), was lieutenant governor of Virginia (an office which made him administrative head of the colony), which no doubt aided their business interests. Lawrence was a partner in the Port Glasgow Rope and Duck Works and also, with Robert, set up the Delftfield Pottery on Glasgow's Brown Street. Robert owned slaves in Virginia, which he sold on his retirement to London; the Dinwiddies also loaned money, equating to millions in today's terms, to Glasgow Town Council.[107] Germiston House, which stood in the area of housing between Coll Street and Forge Street[108], passed out of the family's ownership in 1819 and was demolished in 1926.

Gilmorehill

The estate and house of Gilmorehill belonged to Robert Bogle (1757-1821) from 1802 and passed to his son Archibald (1801-58).[109] Both were Caribbean merchants and Robert's brothers, George Bogle (1762-1813) and Andrew Bogle (d. 1838), were Jamaican plantation owners. Archibald was joint owner of three plantations (and

Gilmorehill House.

probably a fourth) in Demerara (now part of Guyana), which in total enslaved 658 people in 1834, but his business connections in Trinidad, Demerara and Jamaica were such that he was able to share in compensation awards of over £69,376. He sold Gilmorehill in 1845 and it was eventually demolished in 1870[110] to be replaced by Glasgow University's Bute Hall (the house stood at the south-west of the quadrangle within the hall's grounds).[111]

In 2019 the university unveiled a plaque near the site of the house, recording Bogle's involvement with slavery, the gifts received by the university from those 'who had profited from slavery', and commemorating 'the lives of all those who suffered enslavement'. The same year the university established the Glasgow-Caribbean Centre for Development Research with the University of the West Indies and announced other initiatives for reparations.[112] A number of other members of the Bogle family – both resident in Scotland and Jamaica – were involved in slavery and the slavery-based economy. Bogle Street in Greenock is named after Robert Bogle due to his marriage into the Shaw Stewart family.

Gladstone Street

This street commemorates Prime Minister William Ewart Gladstone (1809-98), whose family wealth was derived from slavery and who, in his early career, was actively pro-slavery, expressing doubt as to whether slavery was 'sinful'.[113] His father, John Gladstone (1764-1851), was a politician and merchant whose fortune was partly based on trade in

Virginia tobacco and he was owner of two estates in Jamaica and three in Demerara (now part of Guyana), with business associations with several others. One of his Demerara estates saw a major rebellion among enslaved people in 1823. At abolition the estates he owned had registered 769 enslaved people (other estimates bring the total to over 2,500) and his compensation payout was the largest to any one individual: over £106,769. Retaining his estates, after abolition their labour force was replaced by indentured workers from India who worked in conditions very similar to their enslaved predecessors.[114] His fortune passed to his children, including William, who politically supported compensation for plantation owners.[115] He later revised his views and in an 1850 speech in Parliament said, 'With regard to the slave trade, I can find no word sufficiently strong to characterise its enormous iniquity. I believe the slave trade to be by far the foulest crime that taints the history of mankind in any Christian or pagan country.'[116] A Rector of Glasgow University, Gladstone's statue stands in George Square. Fasque House at Fettercairn, Aberdeenshire, was the Gladstone family seat until the 1930s.

The walls and one of the towers of Glasgow Castle in the 1780s. The castle served as the archiepiscopal palace for the Bishops of Glasgow. It fell into disrepair in the 1750s and was finally cleared to make way for the Royal Infirmary in 1789. The Cathedral stands in the centre of the drawing with its western towers intact. These were demolished in the nineteenth century because the Victorians thought they were ugly, the shorter consistory tower in 1846 and the taller one in 1848.

Glasgow Cathedral

A number of men who were involved with the slavery-based economy are commemorated or buried at Glasgow Cathedral. A monument to Andrew Cochrane, Virginia tobacco merchant is situated in the nave.[117] The sacristy features two stained-glass windows memorialising Alexander Speirs of Elderslie, Virginia plantation owner. Another stained-glass window commemorates William Stirling, son of Archibald Stirling the younger. Sir James Stirling (c. 1740-1805), banker and Lord Provost of Edinburgh, who spent the early part of his career in the Caribbean, also has a memorial. The slave trader Richard Oswald of Auchencruive is buried in the nave and Andrew Buchanan is memorialised outside the entrance on a stone marking the grave site of his descendants.[118] The first wife of William McDowall I, plantation-owner and Glasgow sugar trader, is also buried at the Cathedral.[119]

Glassford Street

Born in Paisley, tobacco lord John Glassford (1715-83) first went into business in 1742 with his cousin, Archibald Ingram. In 1750[120] he went into the North American tobacco trade and built a business that was supported by a fleet of 25 ships and nine tobacco stores in Maryland.[121] His wealth allowed him to invest in lavish properties, including Shawfield Mansion, which he bought in 1760[122], Dougalston estate near Milngavie, and Whitehill estate to the east of the city. A portrait of Glassford and his family at Shawfield Mansion, featuring a young African boy servant (though he is almost invisible in the painting), is on display in Glasgow's People's Palace; it also features his third wife, the daughter of the Earl of Cromarty, an indication of his social mobility.[123] However, Glassford's business was ruined by the American Revolutionary War and he died with debts of more than £50,000.[124]

Glassford bought Shawfield Mansion from Caribbean sugar merchant and plantation owner William McDowall I of Castle Semple, Lochwinnoch, who had himself brought the property from its original owner, sugar and tobacco merchant Daniel Campbell (c. 1671-1753). Campbell, who also served as the city's MP, had the three-storey mansion built for himself in 1711/12, the first of several houses built in Glasgow in the eighteenth century by tobacco lords, reflecting their huge wealth.

The mansion's position was at the foot of modern Glassford Street, where it meets Argyle Street, facing down Stockwell Street. The architect was Colen Campbell who also built Woodhall House at Calderbank, Lanarkshire, for Daniel Campbell. Woodhall became his principal residence after Shawfield Mansion was severely damaged in 1725 by rioters upset that he had voted for the introduction of a malt tax which increased the price of beer. Shawfield was wrecked but Campbell received financial compensation for this, enough for him to buy the island of Islay.[125] William McDowall I bought Shawfield from Campbell and restored it to become his city residence. Campbell and McDowell died rich, unlike Glassford, although the latter held on to Shawfield, which was sold by his son in 1792 to a builder who demolished it in order to lay out what was originally called Great Glassford Street.[126] A pair of stone sphinxes from the Shawfield gate pillars are in the possession of Glasgow Museums.

Golfhill House.

Golfhill Drive

The estate of Golfhill (originally Goufhill[127]) was in the area of the current St Rollox Business Park.[128] James Dennistoun of Golfhill (1758-1835; not related to the Dennistouns of Colgrain[129]), partner in the Caribbean trading firm Buchanan, Steven & Co., bought the estate and built Golfhill House in 1802[130] – it stood roughly in the area of the Tesco petrol station off Cobden Road. It is likely that Dennistoun's son, Alexander Dennistoun[131] (1790-1874), an MP for Dunbartonshire, received compensation of over £389 in 1837 for 25 enslaved people on a plantation in the Bahamas.[132] In earlier years Alexander worked for his father's firm and married the daughter of a Bahamas plantation owner. In the mid 1800s he bought plots of land around the Golfhill estate and made plans to develop them as a suburb, which eventually became Dennistoun.[133]

Gordon Street

In 1837 No. 48 Gordon Street was the address of Caribbean merchants Wighton, Gray & Co. (later Gray, Roxburgh & Co.). Archibald Graham Lang was a partner[134] and he also had Glasgow addresses at Woodlands Road, Elinbank Crescent, Buchanan Street and Woodburn Place. The street was possibly named after Caribbean merchant John Gordon of Aikenhead.[135]

Greenfield House.

Greenfield Park

Greenfield Park owes its name to Greenfield House and estate, purchased by coalmaster James McNair in 1759 from the wife of George Bogle of Daldowie.[136] He also bought the adjacent Shettleston estate from Robert Bogle. McNair started coal mining on this land, but he was also involved with Caribbean trade and was known to have travelled to Barbados.[137] His descendants owned a sugar house on Ingram Street.

Greenhead Street

The elaborate building at No. 47 Greenhead Street was built in 1846 as Greenhead House, home to cotton mill owner Duncan McPhail.[138] It then came into the ownership of the city council and in 1859 became the premises of Buchanan's Institute, a school for 'destitute children' whose education was paid for with money left to the city for this purpose by Caribbean merchant James Buchanan (1785-1857). Buchanan, a partner in the firm of Dennistoun, Buchanan & Co., based at No. 36 Candleriggs, was working for the firm in Grenada in 1800 and became managing partner of the firm in Kingston, Jamaica, and Rio de Janeiro.[139] James Buchanan and James Dennistoun were co-partners. Buchanan returned to Scotland in 1816, taking up residence at Moray Place, Edinburgh. He retired from the firm after 1825 and increased his fortune by investing in stocks and shares. He died immensely wealthy and is buried in Dean Cemetery, commemorated by a large monument. However, he left large bequests to Glasgow for the establishment of the school and to the Trades and Merchants Houses and the Royal Infirmary.[140] No. 47 Greenhead Street was later Greenview Special School and then St Aidan's Roman Catholic School. It was converted into apartments in 2006.[141]

Hamilton Drive

John Hamilton (1754-1829), a Caribbean merchant, was Lord Provost three times.[142] He purchased the estate of North Park, west of the city centre in 1799.

Hamilton[143] was connected through marriage to the Bogle family of Caribbean merchants and his wife, Helen Hamilton, inherited a shared in Dunkly estate, Vera Parish, Jamaica, which passed to him on her death.[144] His five sons – George, William, Archibald, Robert and John – all shared in the compensation award of over £6,230 for this estate, which was enslaving 286 people at the time of abolition. They also continued the family connections to the slavery-based economy.

George (1786-1851) spent years in Jamaica as a plantation owner and attorney and agent for many others – he is associated with no less than 71 Jamaican estates on the Legacies of British Slavery database[145] – and, besides Dunkly, he shared in awards totalling £11,704 for seven of them, which together enslaved 526 people. He had three children with Martha Bryce, a 'free woman of colour', and yet a contemporary wrote of him '... conniving at the shocking barbarities committed on the estates.' He returned to Scotland and in 1851 was living with his brother Archibald in Lanarkshire.

William (d. 1866) was a partner in Robert Bogle & Co.[146] and Bogle, King. Apart from the award for Dunsky, he also shared in compensation of over £52,819 for that firm's five Demerara estates (now in Guyana) plus a further four in Trinidad, which collectively enslaved 946 people. He inherited North Park and was a Lord Provost.

John died in Jamaica[147] and Robert[148] (d. 1840) was a merchant there, connected to the Bogles' businesses, and owning property on the island and also in Venezuela.

The family seat, North Park House, was demolished in the 1860s to make way for the 'Greek' Thomson-designed terrace of 35-51 Hamilton Drive (another North Park House was built, later becoming the home of BBC Scotland).[149] Great Hamilton Street, opened in the east of the city in 1813 though now gone, was also named after John Hamilton.[150]

Houldsworth Street

Henry Houldsworth[151] (1770-1853) ran a cotton mill in Cheapside Street from 1801. At that time – and until the American Civil War – cotton imported to Britain for use in mills came from slave-owning plantations in the Caribbean, Guyana, Brazil and the American south.[152] By the 1860s nearly 90% of British cotton textiles were made from American cotton. Houldsworth also went into iron production and founded the Coltness Ironworks, Newmains, and the Dalmellington Iron Co.[153]

Househill Park

Just north of Priesthill and by Barrhead Road, this park is on land that once formed the estate of Househill, which from the early-eighteenth century until 1750 belonged to the Blackburn family of merchants who were trading in 'Virginea [sic], Carriby Islands, Barbadoes, New England, St. Christophers, Monserat, and other colonies in America' from the late seventeenth century.[154] This family tradition continued into the nineteenth century as a later member of the family, John Blackburn (1756-1840), was in Jamaica from 1772 to 1805 as a plantation manager and owner, overseeing around 30 plantations. He returned wealthy enough to buy Killearn estate in Stirlingshire, rebuilding Killearn House in grand style, and continued to receive income from plantations that he still partly owned.[155] On abolition he received most of the compensation of over £11,964 paid out for 638 people enslaved on three Jamaican plantations: Spanishtown and Angel's Pen in St Catherine Parish and Wallens and New Works in St Thomas-in-the-Vale Parish.[156] Househill mansion was demolished in the early 1930s.[157]

Ingram Street

Originally Back Cow Lane, Ingram Street was built in 1781[158] and named after Archibald Ingram (1699-1770), tobacco lord and a two-time Lord Provost. He started trading in tobacco in 1720 and from 1742 his partner was his brother-in-law John Glassford, establishing the firm of Ingram & Glassford.[159] He was also a founder of the Pollokshaws Calico Printing Co. and the Inkle Co., which manufactured textiles that were exported back to America in the ships which brought the tobacco.

His son was Archibald Ingram of St Kitts and St Vincent[160] (d. 1778). His firm was Archibald Ingram & Co. of St Kitts and he was also at one time a partner in James Ingram & Co. of Glasgow with George Oswald and John Glassford among others. He was an owner of Ottley Hall[161] plantation, St Vincent (this had 70 people enslaved in 1834) and he was a member of the Council of St Vincent in 1771. At one time resident in Downing Street, London, his will left all his 'plantations . . . negroes or slaves . . .' to his son, Archibald Hyndman Ingram of Stratford.

Ingram the tobacco lord is commemorated by a marble relief structure in the Merchants House[162] and is thought to be buried in Ramshorn Cemetery in the street which takes his name. This also has the grave of John Glassford and Andrew Buchanan.[163]

Jamaica Street

By the 1760s Glasgow's sugar trade with the Caribbean was well established and the name of the key place of production of this commodity was given to this street, which opened in 1763.[164] By this time the city had a number of sugar houses for processing raw sugar in Candleriggs, Gallowgate, King Street and Stockwell Street.

James Watt Street

The Greenock-born mechanical engineer's steam engine was hugely important to industrialisation. He was also involved in the Delftfield Pottery in Brown Street. Before his engineering achievements Watt was involved in his family's colonial merchant business, which included slave trading, and was also involved in the trafficking of an enslaved Afican boy to the Spynie family of Morayshire.

Jordanhill

In existence from the sixteenth century, the estate of Jordanhill was bought by Alexander Houston (1709-77) in 1750. From the 1720s he and his brother William worked for William McDowall I of Castle Semple, Lochwinnoch, in his sugar exporting and processing business (William Houston captained ships carrying this cargo). He went on to establish the Caribbean merchant firm of Alexander Houston & Co. which launched slaving voyages in the 1760s, and in 1789 petitioned the House Commons for the continuation of the African slave trade to maintain the supply of enslaved people to Caribbean plantations.[165] His son, Andrew Houston (d. 1800), continued the business – and built a new mansion at Jordanhill – but the company went bankrupt in 1795.[166] Andrew's son, Robert (1749-1848), continued to own the plantation of Belmont in Grenada and was awarded over £5,024 in compensation for 194 enslaved people in 1835.[167]

Jordanhill House.

In 1800 Archibald Smith (1749-1821) bought Jordanhill estate.[168] As the fourth son of John Smith of Craigend, Stirlingshire – the founder of the Glasgow booksellers John Smith & Son – he was expected to make his own living and travelled with two of his brothers to America, where he became involved in the Virginia and North Carolina tobacco trade, managing a tobacco store.[169] He returned to Scotland on the outbreak of the American Revolutionary War and then went into business as a Caribbean merchant[170], becoming partner in the firm of Leitch and Smith (along with his brothers John and James) which had interests in Jamaica and Grenada. He also founded a Glasgow linen wholesaler and was partner in the cotton manufacturers James Finlay & Co.

On Archibald's death Jordanhill passed to his son James Smith[171] (1782-1867), who continued the family firm with his brother Archibald[172] (b. 1795) as J. & A. Smith. Apparently James was more of a sleeping partner with academic interests while Archibald took a more active role in the business. Both men had other business and civic involvements: Archibald was a major investor in local railways including the Edinburgh and Glasgow Railway and James was a president of Anderson's Institution (also known as Anderson's University), precursor to the University of Strathclyde. In 1836 both men and their co-partner Robert McCunn (whose address was '81 Vincent Street, Glasgow') shared compensation of over £12,573 for 480 people enslaved on six plantations on Grenada. Another of the Smith brothers, William[173] (1787-1871), was also a Caribbean merchant who co-owned the plantation of Jordanhill, Trinidad, sharing in compensation of over £7,649 for the 154 people enslaved there (his home was the mansion of Carbeth Guthrie, near Carbeth in Stirlingshire).

Jordanhill House was demolished in 1961 as part of the development of Jordanhill Teacher Training College.

Keir Street

The Keir estate, near Bridge of Allan, Stirlingshire, was owned by the Stirling family from 1448. The Stirlings were involved in slavery from 1733 when Archibald Stirling the elder (1710-83) tried to make his fortune in Jamaica; he left only two years later and had more success in India. However, with money borrowed from him, his brother Robert (1715-64) went to Jamaica in 1748 and bought Frontier estate (producing sugar and rum) in St Mary Parish. In 1757, jointly with another brother – James (1714-73) – he bought Hampden estate (also producing sugar and rum; the stadium is *not* named after this estate) in St James Parish. 750 people were enslaved on Robert's estates.

Archibald Stirling the younger (1769-1847), nephew of Archibald the elder, spent twenty years on the family's Jamaican estates and, as a beneficiary of awards of over £12,517, was hugely compensated on abolition by the Slave Compensation Commission. He married Elizabeth Maxwell of Nether Pollok (when Archibald's son William assumed the Maxwell baronetcy in 1865 the family name became Stirling-Maxwell). Together they had three children, but he fathered a further six illegitimately, one of whom was Edward Stirling (1804-73), whose mother was a 'creole woman of colour, possibly called Jeanne'; Edward became a significant figure in South Australia politics.[174] Archibald's brother was the Caribbean trader Charles Stirling. William Stirling sold the Jamaican estates in the 1850s.[175]

Kelvingrove House.

Kelvingrove

Kelvingrove House was built in 1783[176] by tobacco and Caribbean merchant and Lord Provost, Patrick Colquhoun (1745-1820). He was born in Dumbarton and went to Virginia as a sixteen year old, working in a tobacco store.[177] He later came back to Scotland, becoming one of the tobacco lords. His firm, Colquhoun & Ritchie, operated in Jamaica and Antigua. This went bankrupt around 1791, 'unable to adapt to new trading conditions' probably created by American independence.[178] He then sold Kelvingrove House to cotton spinner John Pattison[179] and moved to London.

Pattison sold the house in 1795 to Richard Dennistoun (d. 1833), son of James Dennistoun of Colgrain. Richard was partner in the firm of Campbell, Rivers & Co., active in Trinidad, and shared in compensation of over £2,559 for 51 people enslaved on Belvidere sugar plantation there.[180] Richard's brother, Robert Dennistoun (1770-1815), was partner in the Caribbean merchant firm George & Robert Dennistoun & Co., with connections to St Kitts and Trinidad; he was also a founder of the pro-slavery Glasgow West India Association, established in 1807, which promoted the interests of Glasgow's Caribbean merchants.

Kelvingrove House remained with the Dennistouns until 1841 when it was sold to Colin McNaughton, another Glasgow merchant. In 1852 Glasgow Corporation bought the estate and neighbouring Woodlands and began to develop what became Kelvingrove Park. The house, the site of which is within the area of the roller skating rink in Kelvingrove Park[181], was demolished in 1899.[182] Kelvingrove Art Gallery opened two years later.

Kenmure House.

Kenmure Street

The Kenmure estate and house[183], no longer standing, were sited on the grounds of what is now Bishopbriggs Golf Course. Caribbean merchant Charles Stirling owned the estate from 1806 and built the mansion.[184] He then sold it to his brother, Archibald Stirling the younger, also involved in Caribbean trading, though the house became the home of William Stirling (d. 1862). It was the birthplace of Archibald Stirling's son, Sir William Stirling-Maxwell (1818-78).

King Street

King Street Sugar House was established in 1727[185] to process Caribbean sugar. It was connected to Andrew Cochrane. Other partners and investors included Lord Provosts James Buchanan, Andrew Buchanan, Peter Murdoch and John Coulter (also his son, James)[186], as well as merchant John Wallace. There were also sugar houses at Gallowgate, Stockwell Street and Candleriggs.

King's Park

Standing within King's Park, Aikenhead House was built in 1806 and bought two years later by John Gordon (1753-1828), a partner of the Glasgow firm Stirling, Gordon and

Aikenhead House.

Co., which imported sugar from Jamaican plantations[187] (Charles Stirling was a co-partner). Gordon was a chairman of the Glasgow West India Association, which advanced the interests of Glasgow businessmen connected to Caribbean trade and later opposed emancipation and campaigned for compensation for estate owners once this came into force.[188] The house was converted into flats in 1986.[189]

Kingston / Kingston Dock / Kingston Bridge

Named after King George III (1738-1820). Though apparently privately disapproving, he was monarch throughout the period that saw the highest British involvement with the transatlantic slave trade and Caribbean slavery. The dock and bridge were named after the area.[190]

Linn Park / Linn House

Linn estate was established around 1792, formed from land of Hagtonhill estate which had been owned by the McDowalls of Lochwinnoch. There was probably a house there from that time[191] though other sources say it was built by Caribbean merchant Colin Campbell in the early 1820s[192] after his purchase of the estate, which he called 'The Lynn'. Campbell was a partner in the Caribbean merchant firm Colin Campbell & Co. and was also resident in the Netherlands. On abolition he shared the compensation award of over £8,899 for the 165 people enslaved at Sans Souci plantation, British

Lynn House.

Guiana (now Guyana).[193] Campbell's brother, Alexander Campbell of Hallyards (1768-1817), was also a Caribbean merchant and co-founder of John Campbell Senior & Co. Campbell sold the house to the son of another Caribbean merchant, John Gordon, around 1840.[194]

London Road

The south-eastern part of London Road runs through the area of Dalbeth, once site of Dalbeth House. In 1754[195] this was bought by Thomas Hopkirk (d. 1781), a Glasgow tobacco lord.[196] His son James (1749-1835) succeeded to the estate[197] and rebuilt the house. He also continued trading in the slavery-based economy, holding shares in the tobacco merchants Findlay, Hopkirk & Co, and the Caribbean merchants Hopkirk, Cunninghame & Co and Hamilton, Hopkirk & Co.[198] James's son Thomas was a botanist who founded the Glasgow Botanic Gardens. Dalbeth House was sold and became part of a convent. It, along with the convent buildings, were eventually demolished to make way for an extension to Dalbeth Cemetery.[199]

McFarlane Street

This was laid out in 1815 and named after Alexander MacFarlane[200] (1702-55), a graduate of the University of Glasgow and astronomer who became a merchant and plantation owner in Jamaica. He was also involved in the civic life of the island,

Dalbeth House.

becoming an assistant judge and Postmaster General, and used his house in Port Royal as an observatory (he also built another observatory in Kingston). He left his observatory instruments to the university (these were restored by James Watt) and this led to the establishment of the MacFarlane Observatory in 1757[201], the first purpose-built university observatory in Britain. In Jamaica MacFarlane owned over 5,600 acres of land, which included the sugar plantations of Biscany, St Elizabeth Parish, and Serge Island, St Thomas-in-the-East Parish. He died in Kingston, owner of 791 enslaved people and worth over £74,500.[202]

Maryland Drive / Maryland Gardens

Named after James Rowan of Maryland, owner of Bellahouston estate.[203]

McNair Street

James McNair was a coal master who also had some involvement with the Caribbean trade.[204] The McNair family were sugar refiners too and owned sugar houses in Gallowgate and Ingram Street.

Merchant City

Merchant City is the name given to the eastern quarter of the city centre, a rectangle formed by Queen Street, Ingram Street, High Street and Argyle Street. First used by historian Charles Oakley in the 1960s, the term was officially adopted in 1990 – the year that Glasgow was named European City of Culture – as part of an urban renewal project by the city council and the Scottish Development Agency. At the time, the decision attracted criticism from some quarters, including the Workers City Group and novelist James Kelman, for its apparent commemoration of the merchants who made their fortunes from the slavery-based tobacco and sugar trades.[205] The name – and the names of streets such as Glassford, Ingram, Virginia and numerous others included in this book – continues to attract criticism and controversy. At the time of writing, a 'petition to rename Glasgow street names which are named after slave owners' currently has nearly 28,000 signatures.[206] In 2022 Glasgow City Council resolved to make a public consultation on how to address the issue.[207]

Glasgow Tolbooth steeple with one of the Merchant City signposts.

No. 42 Miller Street.

Miller Street

Miller Street was laid out in 1773 and the building now known as the 'Tobacco Merchants' House', No. 42, was built in 1775. Ten years later it became the home of Robert Findlay of Easterhill (1748-1802) who was involved in the Virginia tobacco trade before moving into Caribbean trading after the American Revolutionary War; his son, Robert Junior, continued in this business after his death.[208] Findlay Senior kept the money he made from his business in the house and some of his iron safes are still in the building.[209] The Findlay family owned the building into the 1830s. Today it is the home of the Scottish Civic Trust and can be visited by the public on Doors Open days.

Mitchell Library

The Mitchell Library on North Street opened in 1911. It was originally established in 1877, in premises at the corner of Albion and Ingram streets[210], financed by a bequest from Stephen Mitchell to Glasgow Town Council for the establishment of a 'large Public Library in Glasgow'.[211] Mitchell (1789-1874) was head of the tobacco manufacturing firm Stephen Mitchell & Sons, which was founded in Linlithgow in 1723 and moved to Glasgow in 1825. The business was built on links with the Virginia tobacco trade though Mitchell sold his shares on retirement and invested in other interests.[212]

Monteith Place / Monteith Row

Henry Monteith (1764-1848), a cotton manufacturer, was also an MP and Lord Provost[213] twice. Monteith owned Barrowfield Dye Works at Dalmarnock and also

Bleachfield at the Barrowfield Dye Works.

Blantyre Mill where the explorer and anti-slavery campaigner David Livingstone was employed as young man.[214] Monteith's cotton works were very likely to have used Caribbean cotton as he was associated with Glasgow-based Caribbean merchants[215], one of whom was Robert Bogle.[216]

Moore Street

Sir John Moore (1761-1809) was a lieutenant-general in the British Army who was born in Glasgow and attended Glasgow High School. He was sent to the Caribbean under Sir Ralph Abercromby in 1796 and was a senior officer involved in the retaking of St Lucia from the French, who had repulsed an attempted British invasion the year before. The two countries had been fighting over the island since the 1660s[217] and possession moved between them several times. The French started plantations with slave labour on the island in the 1750s, though in a later period of French rule in the aftermath of the French Revolution enslaved people were set free.[218] The British were determined to take back the island and restore slavery for plantation owners and Moore's army was successful in establishing British control. He was then made governor of the island[219] and remained there until the following year. A treaty in 1802 gave control of St Lucia back to France and Napoleon then re-established slavery under the French.[220] Britain took control again from 1814 and slavery continued until abolition in 1833. Even then, enslaved people had to endure 'apprenticeships' which meant they had to continue working for plantation owners for free for much of their working week.[221] This practice ended in 1838. Moore was killed at the Battle of Corunna in 1809; this street was named after him and a statue of him was also erected in George Square.

Moore Park House.

Moore Park

This estate lay in the area west of Ibrox Stadium that is now an industrial estate, bounded by Edminston Drive to the south, Broomloan Road to the east and Helen Street to the west. Moore Park mansion was built in the early 1800s and it became the home of James Campbell (1792-1874)[222], son of John Campbell who established John Campbell Senior & Co. He was a partner in the company and on abolition shared in compensation amounting to over £78,265 for the loss of labour from 1,484 people enslaved on the companies plantations in British Guiana (now Guyana).[223] The house was demolished in the 1870s and the land was later the site of a housing estate, Moorepark.[224] This was itself demolished in the 1990s and the area is now an industrial estate.

Mount Vernon

Mount Vernon estate had originally been called Windy Edge from at least the early sixteenth century. It was bought by Glasgow merchant Robert Boyd in 1742 and he renamed it in honour of Admiral Edward Vernon[225], famous for a victory in the recent War of Jenkin's Ear in 1708.[226] Vernon had been commander of the Royal Navy's West India station, defending British commercial interests in the area. Tobacco merchant Andrew Buchanan of Drumpellier (1691-1759) bought the estate in 1756. His son George Buchanan (1728-62), also a tobacco trader, later built the house as a country home; his Glasgow residence was Virgina Mansion on Virginia Street. Unlike the latter, Mount Vernon stayed in the family throughout the 1800s. The mansion was pulled down in 1932 to make way for the housing estate named after it.

Mount Vernon House.

Nelson Mandela Place

St George's Parish Church (now St George's Tron Church of Scotland) opened in 1808. Its parishioners included many involved in the slavery-based economy[227], among them Caribbean merchants and members of the Glasgow West India Association John Gordon and James Ewing. The church stands in what was originally St George's Place, also the former site of the South African Consulate.[228] In 1986 the city council changed the name to honour Nelson Mandela, the first city in the world to make this gesture, but also gave the name 'Merchant City' to the area just east of this church four years later. Nelson Mandela Place also features a statue of James Watt above the entrance to the Atheneum Building.[229]

Nelson Street / Nelson Street

Nelson Street, Baillieston, Nelson Street, Tradeston and the Merchant City's lost Nelson Street – which became the southern end of Albion Street – are named after the Royal Navy admiral and British national hero Horatio Nelson (1758-1805), who spent part of his naval career in the 1770s and 80s in the Caribbean. In 1784 he was tasked with enforcing the Navigation Acts (which regulated trading among Britain's Caribbean possessions, all involved in the slavery-based economy). While there, he met Frances ('Fanny') Nisbet, the daughter of a Nevis plantation owner, marrying her on the island in 1787. There is some debate over Nelson's views on slavery. A letter written by him to a plantation owner appears to defend the possession of Caribbean colonies and also to attack William Wilberforce[230], though the Nelson Society, among others, disputes that Nelson held pro-slavery or racist views.[231]

Northwoodside House.

North Park Street

Named after the estate of Caribbean merchant and Lord Provost, John Hamilton.

North Woodside Road

The Northwoodside estate was once in this area and belonged in the 1760s and 70s to Caribbean merchant Archibald Stirling of Kier. It was subsequently owned by another Caribbean merchant, James Lapsley.[232] Lapsley feued the land at Kelvinbridge to William Gillespie, who established a cotton mill powered by the River Kelvin. In 1799 he employed Henry Houldsworth (see *Houldsworth Street*) as manager of the mill, and sold it to him two years later. William Gillespie built Northwoodside House, which was enlarged in the early nineteenth century by his son Colin, referred to by Smith and Mitchell as an 'American merchant'.[233] The house was demolished in 1869.[234] The northern end of Belmont Bridge is on its site.

Oswald Street

James Oswald of Shieldhall (1779-1853) served as an MP for the city[236] though the street was named before the time of his public service; when it was laid out it bordered land that he owned.[236]

Pitt Street

William Pitt (1759-1806) twice served as Prime Minister of Great Britain. He was a friend of William Wilberforce and on the issue of the slave trade made clear he was against it. As Prime Minister, in 1792 he pressed Parliament to abolish it: 'We may now consider this trade as having received its condemnation; that its sentence is sealed; that this Curse of mankind is seen by the House in its true light; and that the greatest stigma on our national character which ever existed, is about to be removed!'[237] However, the trade was not abolished until 1807 and during his premierships the British government became the world's biggest buyer of enslaved people, many to become soldiers in British Army regiments in the Caribbean.[238]

Plantation / Plantation Park / Plantation Square / Plantation Park Gardens / Plantation Quay

The Plantation district, north of Kinning Park, originated as the Craigiehall estate, the name being changed by Caribbean merchant John Robertson after he bought it in 1783.[239] He sold the estate ten years later (apparently his estate was sequestered in 1792)[240] but the name was retained and has persisted, even though the estate and mansion have been gone since the late nineteenth century. In 1793 Robertson was a co-owner of Prospect estate, Grenada, which at that time enslaved 150 people.[241] Through one of his business dealings, Roberton's son, John Murdoch Robertson (1777-1848), was later able to benefit from half the compensation award for Mount Pleasant estate, St Vincent, which at the time of abolition enslaved 231 people.[242]

Plantation House.

Pollok House

The estate of Nether Pollok was owned by the Maxwell family for over 700 years. Pollok House was completed in 1752 and both house and estate were given by the family to the City of Glasgow in 1966, with the subsequent creation of Pollok Park. The Maxwells became involved in slavery from the mid-eighteenth century – Sir Walter Maxwell (1732-62) was likely to have had some connection to the slave trade[243] and his brother, James Maxwell (1735-85), went to St Kitts to work on a plantation owned by Robert Colhoun (or Colquhoun), who had himself started out as an overseer of a plantation owned by William McDowall I of Lochwinnoch. (Colhoun was grandson of one of the first Scots to establish a plantation in the Caribbean in the mid-seventeeth century.)

James became heir to Nether Pollok and married Colhoun's daughter; the couple benefited greatly from inheriting her father's business interests.[244] In the nineteenth century, James's granddaughter married into the Stirling family, her husband Archibald Stirling the younger having spent years in Jamaica overseeing his family's plantations there. The family – renamed the Stirling-Maxwells – received compensation of over £12,000 on abolition for the loss of 690 enslaved people. Naturally this money was inherited by its heirs, though it is not yet clear from research how much money derived from the profits of slavery contributed to Pollok House, its art collection and the development of the estate.[245] Auldhouse and Haggs Castle were other houses owned by the Maxwells in the period of their connections to the slavery-based economy.

Pollok House.

Auldhouse.

Haggs Castle.

Masts project above the buildings of Port Dundas, drawn by Joseph Swan from Garnet Hill in the late 1820s.

Port Dundas / Dundashill / Dundas Lane / Dundas Street / Dundasvale Court

Port Dundas was built between 1786 and 1790 as the terminus of a branch of the Forth & Clyde Canal and was named after Sir Lawrence Dundas (1712-81), who was governor of the Forth & Clyde Navigation Co.[246] First Baronet of Kerse, near Falkirk, he was a major British landowner and also owned plantation estates, one in Grenada and one in Dominica.[247] The latter was Castle Bruce[248], which at the time of abolition enslaved 162 people. For the loss of the slave labour of these people, Dundas's grandson, Lawrence Dundas, 1st Earl of Zetland (1766-1839)[249], shared in compensation of over £3,317. He also shared in compensation of over £4,818 for the 187 people enslaved on Dougalston estate, Grenada, which may have been his grandfather's property there (Sir Thomas Dundas, son of Sir Lawrence of Dundas of Kerse and father of Lawrence, 1st Earl of Zetland, was registered as owner of it in 1820).[250]

Dundas House in St Andrew Square, Edinburgh, was built as a town house for Sir Lawrence Dundas of Kerse. It is now the registered office of the Royal Bank of Scotland.

Possilpark / Possil Road

In 1808 the estate of Possil was purchased (or possibly inherited) by Alexander Campbell (1780-1849), son of Caribbean sugar merchant, John Campbell Senior

Possil House.

(c. 1735-1807), founder of the firm John Campbell Senior. & Co., in which a number of his relatives were partners and which owned plantation estates in British Guiana (now Guyana), Carriacou, Grenada, Trinidad and St Vincent.[251] Not only did the family profit from the slavery-based economy while slavery was legal, they continued to do so by claiming tens of thousands of pounds worth of compensation for the loss of enslaved labourers in the years after abolition. Alexander Campbell[252] was the sole recipient of over £6,113 of compensation for the 232 people enslaved on Mount Rose estate in St Patrick Parish, Grenada.[253] The firm ended in 1858 and within twenty years Possil House and its estate had gone, replaced by the iron foundry of William McFarlane & Co., who also built houses for foundry workers, forming the suburb of Possilpark.[254] Archibald Alison, after whom Allison Street was possibly named, was a resident of the house.

Queen Street

The site of Crawford Mansion – city home to Caribbean plantation owner James Ewing (1775-1853). In 1842 the mansion was replaced by Queen Street Station.[255]

Rodney Street

Admiral George Bridges Rodney (1718-92) was the naval commander responsible for the taking of Martinique, St Lucia and Grenada in 1762, enabling the establishment of British colonies which became dependent on slave labour.[256]

Robertson Street

Originally named Madeira Street, this was renamed after Caribbean merchant John Robertson, who was a partner in the Smithfield Ironworks company which was based there from the 1730s.[257] From the latter half of the seventeenth century, Scotland was connected to the Madeira wine trade[258] and the island became an important stopping-point for British ships engaged in the 'triangular trade' between Britain, Africa and North America, including the Caribbean. Madeira was a Portuguese possession from the fifteenth century and, before wine became its principal export, until the end of the sixteenth century it was a major producer of sugar from plantations using enslaved labourers from Africa.[259] Slavery was abolished there from 1767.[260]

Royal Exchange Square

The square is dominated by the Gallery of Modern Art, which opened in 1996. This building originated as the Cunninghame Mansion, built in 1778 for tobacco lord William Cunninghame (1731-99). Cunninghame was in Virginia working for the Glasgow firm of Cochrane, Murdoch & Co. from the 1740s, returning to Scotland in 1762 and eventually gaining control of the company and renaming it William Cunninghame & Co.[261] It became one of the main importers of tobacco and, having stockpiled the commodity, Cunninghame made huge profits from selling it after war

The Cunninghame Mansion, drawn by Joseph Swan c. 1828. In 1789 William Cunninghame sold the house to John Stirling who lived there until 1817 when he sold it to the Royal Bank of Scotland. It built the curved stairs to the first floor drawing room where the bank tellers worked. The bank sold the building in 1827 to the subscribers of the Royal Exchange. The columned building on the right was the Theatre Royal. Built in 1805, it lasted until 1829 when it was gutted by fire.

broke out in America. Later, he became involved in the Caribbean trade though he made substantial losses from this.

In the 1820s the mansion became the Royal Exchange, meeting place of the Glasgow West India Association.[262] For this use, Corinthian columns were built at the Queen Street entrance, along with the cupola above, among other additions.

The equestrian statue of the Duke of Wellington in front of the Queen Street entrance was unveiled in 1844. After his military career, the duke entered politics, serving as Prime Minister twice, from 1828 to 1830 and in 1834. In 1814, as British Ambassador to France, he attempted to negotiate an end to that country's slave trade and corresponded with William Wilberforce.[263] In a House of Lords debate in 1833 he claimed of himself 'that he had done more in the way of negotiation, written more notes, and entered into more treaties on the subject of the abolition of the slave trade, and of putting an end to slavery than any man living.'[264] However, he was a defender of the interests of Caribbean plantation owners facing the prospect of abolition and has been described as 'the most ardently pro-slavery politician of the 19th century'.[265]

Royal Exchange Square in 2023. The Cunninghame Mansion forms part of the building in the centre of the square but is covered by the colonnaded façade of the Royal Exchange which is now GoMA (Gallery of Modern Art). The Duke of Wellington is wearing his traditional traffic cone, and has several spares on the statue's plinth. The cone's presence secured the street artist Banksy's first exhibition in 14 years, in 2023, drawn by the folk art that has adorned the statue since at least the 1980s. A Banksy mural entitled 'Slave Labour', which originally appeared on the wall of a London Poundland store, was interpreted as a condemnation of the use of child labour in sweatshops.

Ruchill House.

Ruchill

This district is named after the estate in the area which belonged to the Peadie family from the mid-seventeenth century.[266] James Peadie was Lord Provost in 1691/92 and 1697/98[267] and was a partner in the Easter Sugar House, Gallowgate.[268] Ruchill House was built for him around 1700.[269] It was later significantly extended and from 1824 was owned by Isabella Bryson Dennistoun, daughter of Caribbean merchant James Dennistoun of Colgrain.[270] The house was demolished around the time of the First World War.[271]

St Andrews Square

This address is dominated by St Andrew's in the Square Church (St Andrew's Parish Church), built between 1739 and 1756. It is likely that tobacco merchants contributed towards its construction costs.[272] The buildings of the square around the church were built from 1787 and it became a sought-after address for the merchant elite of the city. The last service in the church was held in 1993.

Sauchiehall Street

'Sauchiehall Road' was recorded as the address of William Mathieson (1741-1846), Caribbean merchant and partner to James Ewing. Along with Ewing, in 1837 Mathieson was awarded over £3,313 for compensation claims on two Jamaican estates, including Minard estate, Saint Ann Parish, which enslaved 136 people. His estate was worth over £24,101 on his death.[273]

Scotstoun

A number of members of the extended Oswald family were involved in the slavery-based economy, the most notorious of whom is probably Richard Oswald (1705-84) of Auchencruive, Ayrshire, who was an owner of the slave trading 'factory' of Bunce Island on the Sierra Leone River. There was, however, another, earlier, Richard Oswald (1687-1766) who preceded him in making money from slavery, and was noted as an expert on it.[274] This Richard and his brother, Alexander Oswald (1694-1763), were Glasgow-based merchants and shipowners who traded in Virginia tobacco as well as goods from Madeira and the Caribbean.[275] Together they bought Scotstoun estate and house in 1751.[276] They also owned Balshagray estate and built a mansion in Stockwell Street known as Oswald's Land.

On Richard's death, Scotstoun (along with Balshagray) passed to his second cousin, George Oswald (1735-1819), a merchant who was partner in the tobacco firm of Oswald, Dennistoun and Co. He was also an owner of Blawarthill estate, a partner in the Glasgow Ship Bank and served as Rector of Glasgow University.[277] He inherited Auchencruive estate from his uncle Richard Oswald in 1784. Scotstoun remained in the Oswald family until the 1860s and was demolished to make way for the Lanarkshire and Dunbartonshire Railway in the 1890s.[278]

Scotstoun House.

Shieldhall House.

Shieldhall

This estate and house was purchased in 1781 by Glasgow merchant Alexander Oswald (1738-1813), a partner in the South Sugar House Company which processed Caribbean sugar. He has been described as a tobacco lord[279]; nonetheless, the lengthy description of Oswald in *The Old Country Houses of the Old Glasgow Gentry* points out that in his business he refused 'West India offers' and 'would not, directly or indirectly mix himself up with slavery.'[280] It seems that while Alexander was prepared to profit from the slavery-based economy, he was careful to avoid direct links with slavery itself.[281]

His son James (1779-1853) inherited the estate and his father's commercially built wealth in 1813 and appears to have continued this ambiguous relationship with slavery. He was a cotton manufacturer who had a major spinning factory at Barrowfield and, after abolition of slavery, as MP for Glasgow appears to have assisted in gaining compensation for city merchants with slave-owning interests.[282] However, he also supported the end of Apprenticeship, the system that replaced slavery which meant that formerly enslaved people still had to work without pay for their former 'masters' for up to six years. He inherited Auchencruive in 1841. Glasgow's Oswald Street was named after him and his statue is in George Square. The site of the estate is now taken by the Shieldhall Industrial Estate.[283]

Speirs Wharf

Tobacco merchant Archibald Speirs was Chairman of Management of the Forth & Clyde Canal.[284] Still standing at the wharf today is the Georgian building of c. 1812[285] which was the offices of the Forth & Clyde Navigation Co.. The adjacent grain mills were not built until the 1850s.

Springbank House.

Springbank Gardens / Springbank Crescent / Springbank Court

These streets are just east of the site, on today's London Avenue,[286] of Springbank House. This was built by James Wardrop who owned the estate from around 1780.[287] On his death in 1783 it passed to his son, also James, who was a tobacco merchant in partnership with his brother John. Their business was ruined by the American Revolutionary War. Caribbean merchant Walter Ewing Maclae of Cathkin House, Rutherglen, was the trustee responsible for winding up Wardrop's bankrupt estate, though the house went to James and John's sister, Isobel, who remained owner until 1806.[288]

Stockwell Street

Site of the South Sugar Works, which processed imported Caribbean sugar. Other Glasgow sugar houses were at Gallowgate, Candleriggs and King Street. The street was also the site of Oswald's Land, a mansion belonging to tobacco merchants Richard and Alexander Oswald. This was built with large cellars for the storage of Virginian tobacco and Madeira wine[289] and was demolished in 1875.

Tobago Street

Tobago Street in Calton stands in an area that was once part of the estate of Barrowfield which was bought in 1730[290], along with Camlachie estate, by Glasgow merchant and Rector of Glasgow University, John Orr (c. 1700-43). In the 1760s John Orr's grandsons – John, Matthew and Thomas – all went to Tobago, along with many

Corner of Stockwell Street and Clyde Street, drawn by William Simpson in 1846. The western wing of the building on the corner became Glasgow's custom house in 1757.

other Scots, after it became a British possession.[291] The main exports from the island's plantations were sugar, cocoa and cotton.[292] Thomas bought land there which became the Belmont estate in St George Parish and he died on the island in 1787.[293] Matthew had interests in the estates of Brotherfield and Sandy River, which he left to John on his death in 1787; he died in 1790 at Kings Bay estate, St Paul Parish, of which John was an owner.[294] John (d. 1803) was also a joint-owner of Montreuil estate, Grenada[295]; he later returned to Glasgow and was Town Clerk.[296] His son Thomas (d. 1817) was also a planter on Tobago.[297] Possession of the island passed to the French but it returned to British control after Abercromby's campaign in the 1790s. Tobago Street was likely to have been given its name at that time.[298]

Trongate

From 1787 this was the address of the Caribbean trading firm John Hamilton & Co.[299], owned by John Hamilton of North Park. Trongate was where the Glasgow Tontine Society opened its hotel, coffee room and reading room in 1784.[300] The society existed until 1861, its members coming from Glasgow's merchant class, including John Glassford.[301] There was a piazza there that became a favourite place for tobacco lords to discuss business. The hotel burned down in 1911. The name lives on in the Tontine Building at No. 20 Trongate and in Tontine Lane/Close leading off Trongate.

The Trongate in 1774.

Turnbull Street

This street is the site of St Andrews by the Green Church, built in 1750[302] and known as the 'Whistlin' Kirk' as it was the first church in Glasgow to have an organ.[303] The Virginia tobacco merchants Richard and Alexander Oswald helped to establish the church. Its parishioners later included Caribbean merchants such as Charles Stirling.[304] The church is well preserved and now contains the offices of the Glasgow Association of Mental Health.

University of Glasgow

In the eighteenth and nineteenth centuries the University of Glasgow, at first based in High Street, received funds from a number of bequests from Caribbean merchants and others connected to the slavery-based economy. In 2018 the university commissioned a report into its links with slavery and this estimated that the present-day value of these funds may have exceeded £198 million.[305] Among the merchants making gifts to the university was James Ewing. Bute Hall in the later West End campus stands on land that belonged to Caribbean merchants Robert and Archibald Bogle. The university produced many graduates who went on to make fortunes in the slavery-based economy (e.g. Jamaican plantation owner Alexander MacFarlane) and was served by Rectors involved in it (e.g. George Bogle). However, it also had staff who campaigned against slavery and the senate petitioned Parliament twice in the late 1700s against slavery. Since its 2018 report, the university has established the Glasgow-Caribbean Centre for Development Research with the University of the West Indies and announced other initiatives for reparations.[306]

The High Street looking south to the Tolbooth steeple, drawn by J. Knox in the late 1820s. On the left are the buildings of Glasgow University which moved from here to Gilmorehill in the 1870s.

The Hunterian Museum, Library and Common Hall of the High Street Glasgow University, drawn from the College Gardens by John Fleming, c. 1828.

University of Strathclyde

The University of Strathclyde's history begins in 1796 when the Andersonian Institute (aka Anderson's Institution) was formed with a bequest from the will of John Anderson, professor of Natural Philosophy at the University of Glasgow, to create a second university in the city. Between 1830 and 1844[307] the president of Anderson's University, as it was by then known, was James Smith, sleeping partner in a Caribbean merchant firm. After abolition Smith shared in substantial compensation for the loss of enslaved labour on six Grenadan plantations. In 2021 the university indicated that it would be assessing its archives to determine what links may exist between the Andersonian and the slavery-based economy of the eighteenth and nineteenth centuries.[308]

Virginia Street / Virginia Place / Virginia Court / Virginia Buildings

Virginia Street was laid out by 1753 on land owned by Lord Provost Andrew Buchanan (1691-1759) and named after the place from which he made his fortune. Buchanan and his brothers established the firm of Andrew Buchanan, Bros. & Co., owning their own ships and plantations in Virginia, and becoming the largest tobacco importer in Glasgow. Buchanan was also involved with the King Street Sugar House.[309]

His main residence was Drumpellier House in countryside east of the city (the estate now forms Drumpellier Country Park, Coatbridge). His son, George Buchanan, continued the family business and built Virginia Mansion in the area of Virginia Place. The mansion was sold in 1770 to tobacco merchant Alexander Speirs.[310] In 1793 it was probably bought by John Dunlop, a Lord Provost and son of tobacco lord Colin Dunlop.[311] It was pulled down in the 1840s and replaced by elaborate premises for the

Drumpellier House.

Glasgow Ship Bank[312], of which Andrew Buchanan had been a founder. This building is now home to the Corinthian Club.

West Campbell Street

Glasgow MP Archibald Campbell supported the Glasgow West India Association in Parliament.[313]

West George Street

Named after George III, from 1818 this was the site of a Congregationalist chapel whose minister, the Rev. Dr Ralph Wardlaw (1779-1853), along with William Smeal (1792-1877), helped to found the Glasgow Anti-Slavery Society in 1822.[314] Wardlaw is buried at the Glasgow Necropolis; David Livingstone attended his sermons. The chapel stood close to Queen Street Station and was demolished in 1975.[315]

Whitehill Street / Whitehill Gardens / Whitehill Place

The estate of Whitehill was formed by tobacco lord John Glassford from lands he purchased from the Merchants House in the mid-eighteenth century.[316] Glassford built the mansion but sold it and the estate in 1759 to another Virginia tobacco merchant, John Wallace (1712-1805).[317] Wallace was a partner in the King Street Sugar House [318] and also a major owner of sugar plantations in Jamaica. He sold the house on in 1782 and it was eventually demolished in the late nineteenth century.

Whitehill House.

Yoker

Tobacco lord Alexander Speirs was an owner of this estate.[319]

Yorkhill

This was the western part of the larger lands of Over Newton, jointly owned by George Bogle of Daldowie, who sold off parcels of it in 1777.[320] Around 1800 Yorkhill and also nearby Thornbank House (which stood on the site of today's Centurion Way)[321] were bought by Robert Fulton Alexander (c. 1767-1843) who built Yorkhill mansion in 1805. He sold the estate in 1813. Alexander was a Caribbean merchant and a member of the Glasgow West India Association.[322] The buildings of the Royal Hopsital for Sick Children were built on the site of the estate and mansion.[323]

Yorkhill House.

Bearsden

Kilmardinny House

Around 1800 Caribbean merchant John Leitch (d. 1806), partner in the firm of Leitch & Smith, bought the estate of Kilmardinny.[324] Among a number of interests, including the importing of Jamaican and Grenadan cotton, the firm made business loans to Scottish planters in Jamaica.[325] The estate remained in the Leitch family until 1833[326], when it was sold to 'oil and colour' merchant William Brown (1792-1884). Brown's brothers, Francis (d. 1825) and Robert (1789-1873), were plantation owners in St Vincent and Trinidad, businesses which passed on to other members of the family, some of whom were compensated for the loss of slave labour after abolition. William Brown[327] himself received a third of the compensation of over £7,649 paid out for the 154 people who had been enslaved on Jordan Hill estate in Trinidad. Kilmardinny House is now a wedding and events venue owned by East Dunbartonshire Council.[328]

Kilmardinny House.

Cadder House.

Bishopbriggs

Cadder

Cadder (Cawdor) House was built in 1654 and is now the clubhouse of Cawder Golf Club. It was owned by John Stirling (1768-93) who inherited Hampden estate, Jamaica, from his uncle, Archibald Stirling the elder of Keir House, Bridge of Allan, Stirlingshire (this estate is not connected to the stadium in Glasgow). After John Stirling died, his brother, Charles Stirling (1772-1830), had a life rent on the house, living there from 1816 until his own death.[329] Charles was partner in Caribbean trading firm Stirling Gordon & Co. and a founder in 1807 of the Glasgow West India Association which advanced the interests of slavery-dependent trade.[330] Before Cadder House, Charles's residence was Kenmure House, previously owned by Archibald Stirling the younger, who owned Jamaican plantations. Cawder Golf Club has the Keir course, the name derived from the Keir estate.

Clarkston

Greenbank House

This was built around 1763 for Robert Allason (1721-85). The son of a Gorbals baker, Allason was himself initially a baker by trade and based in Port Glasgow. By the 1750s he had become a sugar and tobacco merchant, arranging the shipment of these commodities from the Caribbean and America with return voyages carrying Scottish goods. One of his brothers captained his trading ships while two other brothers were his trading agents in Virginia (the correspondence of one of these brothers, William, survives, giving extensive insight into the business interests built on slavery at this time). Allason's ships also made voyages from West Africa, carrying hundreds of enslaved people to the Caribbean – 149 deaths among them on the 'middle passage' were recorded.

His business was ruined by the American Revolutionary War and he became bankrupt and had to sell Greenbank in 1782. He then lived at Williamwood House, Clarkston, until his death in 1785.[331] He is buried at the cemetery surrounding New Parish Church, Port Glasgow.

Greenbank then passed through a series of owners, including Maitland Hutchison (who died there in 1795), son of Jamaican planter Alexander Hutchison of Southfield, Newton Mearns.[332] In 1790 Maitland was recorded as owner of Reading Pen plantation, St Elizabeth Parish, Jamaica. Under different ownership, in 1836 this plantation had 42 people enslaved, and compensation of over £1,066 was paid to Duncan Robertson of Carronvale House, Falkirk. Since 1976 Greenbank has been in the care of the National Trust for Scotland.

Greenbank House.

Williamwood House

The original Williamwood House was built on the estate of that name which was formed in the 1660s.[333] Sugar and tobacco merchant Robert Allason rented the house after he lost his home of Greenbank through bankruptcy. James Stewart, a partner in the cotton spinning firm of James Finlay & Co., lived there in the 1810s (Caribbean merchant John Gordon was also a partner of that firm).[334] The house was replaced twice; the current incarnation was built in the 1930s.

Cambuslang

Rosebank House.

Rosebank

Rosebank House stood in the area of Cambuslang Park and Ride which is situated between Bridge Street and Rosebank Gardens.[335] It was the country residence of tobacco lord John Murdoch (1709-76) and by the end of the eighteenth century was in the possession of John Dunlop (d. 1820)[336], son of Colin Dunlop, who is also likely to have owned Virginia Mansion after Alexander Spiers. He has been described as a tobacco lord[337] and was a 'collector of customs' at Greenock.[338] Rosebank was then home to David Dale (1739-1806), an entrepreneur of the cotton-spinning industry who founded the cotton mills at New Lanark.[339] He was also secretary[340] for the Glasgow Committee for the Abolition of the Slave Trade, an offshoot of the London-based Society for the Abolition of the Slave Trade that was established in 1787.[341]

Dougalston House.

Milngavie

Dougalston

South-east of Milngavie, from 1761 this area – which contains Dougalston Avenue and Dougalston Gardens – was the country estate of tobacco lord John Glassford, who created Dougalston Loch.[342] He died at the estate in 1783. Dougalston House stood in the vicinity of the homes of Ewing Walk. The factor's house – built in 1770 and now called Glassford House[343] – is nearby and is used for holiday let accommodation.

James Watt Road

Named for the engineer who spent time working in the tobacco trade and who was known to have trafficked an African child. At Milngavie he designed and built a bleachfield, with associated water courses and machinery, for James MacGregor, who owned Clober House which stood in the area between this road and Blackwood Road to its north from 1773 until demolition in the 1960s.[344]

Mains Park

This and the surrounding houses are sited on land that once formed part of Mains estate. Until the 1800s this was called Balvie and was part of the Dougalston estate which was owned by tobacco lord John Glassford and his family from 1767 to 1819.[345]

Balvie House.

Newton Mearns

Southfield House

Situated around seven miles south of Glasgow, this house came into the ownership of Alexander Hutchison (1725-1788) in 1771.[346] He was a planter in Jamaica and his son, Maitland Hutchison, also owned enslaved people there.[347] Southfield remained in the Hutchison family until 1902 and was sold and demolished for the building of Mearnskirk Hospital, which opened in 1930. The hospital buildings were in turn demolished or converted into housing; the present Southfield House – built as part of the hospital complex – remains standing and is the premises of a nursery.[348]

Rutherglen

Cathkin House

Built in 1799 for Walter Ewing Maclae (d. 1814), a Caribbean merchant whose sons were James Ewing of Strathleven (1774-1853) and Humphrey Ewing Maclae (1773-1860). Both followed their father into the trade with considerable success. Humphrey owned three Jamaican plantations – Port Royal (with 161 enslaved people), St Ann (195 enslaved) and Lillyfield (93 enslaved) – and claimed over £8,375 compensation for these in 1835/36. He was resident in Cathkin House from 1814 to 1860.[349] His cousin was anti-slavery campaigner, the Rev. Dr Ralph Wardlaw.

Cathkin House.

Shawfield

From 1707 Shawfield was the country estate of tobacco and sugar merchant Daniel Campbell[350], who built Shawfield Mansion in the area of Glasgow that later became Glassford Street. He retired to the estate after his town house was wrecked by rioters in the Shawfield Riots of 1725. The house and estate remained in the Campbell family until 1788. It stood on the land overlooking the west bank of the Clyde which is now taken by industrial units off Glasgow Road, Rutherglen.

Shawfield House.

REFERENCES

17. J. Rickard, 'Sir Ralph Abercromby, 1734-1801', 19.3.2008, *Historyofwar.org*: http://www.historyofwar.org/articles/people_abercromby_ralph.html
18. *Glasgow, Slavery and Atlantic Commerce*, p. 60.
19. *Glasgow, Slavery and Atlantic Commerce*, p.103.
20. 'Colonel John Gerard', *LBS database*: http://wwwdepts-live.ucl.ac.uk/lbs/person/view/2146630404
21. 'Sir Archibald Alison 1st Bart.', *LBS database*: http://wwwdepts-live.ucl.ac.uk/lbs/person/view/46692
22. *Glasgow, Slavery and Atlantic Commerce*, p. 77.
23. 'Buck's head Hotel', *TheGlasgowStory*: https://www.theglasgowstory.com/image/?inum=TGSA03551&t=2
24. *Lost Glasgow* Facebook page, 23.8.2016: https://en-gb.facebook.com/lostglasgowofficial/posts/929465840498606:0
25. 'When West Was Best', *Lost Glasgow*: https://www.lostglasgow.scot/posts/when-west-was-best-98/
26. Dr Anthony Lewis, 'The Black House', 4.2.2020, *Legacies of Slavery*: https://glasgowmuseumsslavery.co.uk/2020/02/04/the-black-house/
27. 'Black House', *TheGlasgowStory*: https://www.theglasgowstory.com/image/?inum=TGSE00913&t=2
28. Stuart McLean, 'The Oswalds of Scotstoun', 2005, *Jordanhill Local History*: http://www.wsmclean.com/Oswalds.htm
29. 'James Rowan of Bellahouston', 2.5.2022, *Geni*: https://www.geni.com/people/James-Rowan-of-Bellahouston/6000000026294436744
30. *Glasgow, Slavery and Atlantic Commerce*, p. 111.
31. 'Moses Steven', *LBS database*: http://wwwdepts-live.ucl.ac.uk/lbs/person/view/2146667135.
32. 'Glasgow, Bellahouston Park, Bellahouston House', *Canmore*: https://canmore.org.uk/site/160667/glasgow-bellahouston-park-bellahouston-house.
33. *Glasgow, Slavery and Atlantic Commerce*, p. 103.
34. Dr Anthony Lewis, 'The Black House', 4.2.2020, Dr Anthony Lewis, *Legacies of Slavery*:https://glasgowmuseumsslavery.co.uk/2020/02/04/the-black-house/
35. 'Belvidere House', *Old Country Houses*: http://www.glasgowwestaddress.co.uk/Old_Country_Houses/Belvidere.htm
36. *Glasgow, Slavery and Atlantic Commerce*, pps. 80-81.
37. 'Mungo Nutter Campbell', *LBS database*: http://wwwdepts-live.ucl.ac.uk/lbs/person/view/41620
38. 'Belvidere House', *TheGlasgowStory*: https://www.theglasgowstory.com/image/?inum=TGSB00239
39. 'History of the Congregation', 2022, *Blawarthill Parish Church*: https://www.blawarthillchurch.org/history
40. George Manzor, 'Alexander Speirs – Tobacco Lord (1714 – 1782) Part 2', 14.5.2020, *Glasgow's Benefactors*: https://glasgowbenefactors.com/2020/05/14/alexander-speirs-tobacco-lord-1714-1782-part-2/
41. *Glasgow, Slavery and Atlantic Commerce*, p. 61.
42. 'Merchants' Steeple', *TheGlasgowStory*: https://www.theglasgowstory.com/image/?inum=TGSB00085
43. 'Merchants House History Film', 2018, *The Merchant's House of Glasgow*: https://merchantshouse.org.uk/history/
44. *Glasgow, Slavery and Atlantic Commerce*, p. 36.
45. 'The Merchants House of Glasgow Response to Historical Slavery', *The Merchants House of Glasgow*: https://merchantshouse.org.uk/the-merchants-house-of-glasgow-response-to-historical-slavery
46. 'Delftfield Pottery' (2023), *Scottish Pottery Society*: https://www.scottishpotterysociety.org.uk/delftfield/
47. Gerard Ferry, 'Tobacco warehouse frontage, James Watt Street, Glasgow, Scotland, UK', 28.2.2019, *Alamy.com*: https://www.alamy.com/tobacco-warehouse-frontage-james-watt-street-glasgowscotlanduk-image239024154.html
48. Bruce Gittings et al, Andrew Buchanan 1725 – 1783', 2021, *Gazetteer for Scotland*: https://www.scottish-places.info/people/famousfirst4520.html and *Glasgow, Slavery and Atlantic Commerce*, p. 104.
49. 'Glasgow, Baillieston Road, Calder Park House', *Canmore*: https://canmore.org.uk/site/160187/glasgow-baillieston-road-calder-park-house
50. 'Calder Park', *Old Country Houses*: http://www.glasgowwestaddress.co.uk/Old_Country_Houses/Calder_Park.htm
51. *Glasgow, Slavery and Atlantic Commerce*, pp. 97-98.
52. 'Glasgow, 50 Commercial Road, New Adelphi Mill View from SSE showing SW front and ESE front of corner block of New Adelphi Mill with Hosiery Works in background', *Canmore*: https://canmore.org.uk/collection/634768
53. 'Calderpark', *Old Country Houses*: http://www.glasgowwestaddress.co.uk/Old_Country_Houses/Calder_Park.htm
54. *Glasgow, Slavery and Atlantic Commerce*, p. 76.
55. Ibid., p. 87.
56. Ibid., p. 104.
57. 'Tollcross', *Old Country Houses*: http://www.glasgowwestaddress.co.uk/Old_Country Houses/Tollcross.htm

58. 'Royal African Company', 2022, *Wikipedia*: https://en.wikipedia.org/wiki/Royal_African_Company#cite_note-20, quoting Voyages Database: www.slavevoyages.org.
59. 'Royal African Company', 2022, *Wikipedia*: https://en.wikipedia.org/wiki/Royal_African_Company#cite_note-20, quoting Juliet Gardiner, *The History Today Who's Who In British History*, 2000. Collins & Brown Limited and Cima Books. p. 192.
60. 'Craigton House', *TheGlasgowStory*: https://www.theglasgowstory.com/image/?inum=TGSB00258
61. Henry Ritchie', *LBS database*: http://wwwdepts-live.ucl.ac.uk/lbs/person/view/14520
62. *Glasgow, Slavery and Atlantic Commerce*, p. 104.
63. Ibid., p. 59.
64. Ibid., p. 105
65. Ibid., p. 104.
66. 'Cowlairs', *Old Country Houses*: http://www.glasgowwestaddress.co.uk/Old_Country_Houses/Cowlairs.htm
67. 'Michael Scott and James Bogle', *The Friends of Glasgow Necropolis*: https://www.glasgownecropolis.org/profiles/michael-scott-and-james-bogle/
68. Lucy K. Hayden, 'The Caribbean Presence in Tom Cringle's Log: A Commentary on Britain's Involvement in Slavery and the Slave Trade', *Journal of Caribbean Studies*, 6, 3 (Autumn 1988), p. 311.
69. 'Michael Scott of 'Tom Cringle's Log'', *Legacies of Slavery*: http://wwwdepts-live.ucl.ac.uk/lbs/person/view/2146651295
70. 'Cowlairs House', *TheGlasgowStory*: https://www.theglasgowstory.com/image/?inum=TGSB00253&t=2
71. 'Craigpark House', *Old Country Houses*: http://www.glasgowwestaddress.co.uk/Old_Country_Houses/Craigpark_House.htm
72. *Glasgow, Slavery and Atlantic Commerce*, p. 105.
73. John Donoghue, The curse of Cromwell: revisiting the Irish slavery debate', 2017, *History Ireland*: https://www.historyireland.com/curse-cromwell-revisiting-irish-slavery-debate
74. 'George Bogle of Daldowie', *University of Glasgow – The University of Glasgow Story*: https://www.universitystory.gla.ac.uk/biography/?id=WH1143&type=P&o=&start=0&max=20&l=
75. 'Tontine Rooms', *It Wisnae Us*: https://it.wisnae.us/tontine-rooms/
76. 'Daldowie House', *TheGlasgowStory*: https://www.theglasgowstory.com/image/?inum=TGSB00261&t=2
77. *Glasgow, Slavery and Atlantic Commerce*, pp. 105-106.
78. 'James Buchanan of Dowanhill', *LBS database*: http://wwwdepts-live.ucl.ac.uk/lbs/person/view/2146642453
79. 'Records of Dowanhill Estate Co Ltd, property managers, Glasgow, Scotland', *JISC Archives Hub*: https://archiveshub.jisc.ac.uk/search/archives/b0116cbc-1bab-3b75-8cd8-53b3be16db35
80. 'Dowanhill', *Wikipedia*: https://en.wikipedia.org/wiki/Dowanhill, quoting Gordon Urquhart, *Along Great Western Road*, 2000, Stenlake Publishing Ltd.
81. 'Tollcross', *Old Country Houses*: http://www.glasgowwestaddress.co.uk/Old_Country_Houses/Tollcross.htm
82. *Glasgow, Slavery and Atlantic Commerce*, p. 106.
83. 'Glasgow, Carmyle, General', *Canmore*: https://canmore.org.uk/site/78325/glasgow-carmyle-general
84. *Glasgow, Slavery and Atlantic Commerce*, p. 94.
85. 'Easterhill House', *TheGlasgowStory*: https://www.theglasgowstory.com/image/?inum=TGSB00265&t=2
86. 'Glasgow, Easterhill House', *Canmore*: https://canmore.org.uk/site/163705/glasgow-easterhill-house
87. Ibid.
88. Jim Powell, 'Valiant Voice: Charles James Fox', 4.7.2000, *Libertarianism.org*: https://www.libertarianism.org/publications/essays/valiant-voice-charles-james-fox
89. Ibid.
90. *Glasgow, Slavery and Atlantic Commerce*, p. 59.
91. 'Benjamin Franklin's Anti-Slavery Petitions to Congress', *National Archives – The Centre for Legislative Archives*: https://www.archives.gov/legislative/features/franklin#:~:text=As%20a%20young%20man%20he,slavery%20in%20his%20private%20correspondence
92. *Glasgow, Slavery and Atlantic Commerce*, p. 105.
93. David Leask, 'Glasgow – a monument to barons of slave trade', 12.2.22, *The Herald*: https://www.heraldscotland.com/news/19988640.big-read-glasgow---monument-barons-slave-trade/
94. *Glasgow, Slavery and Atlantic Commerce*, p. 37.
95. Ibid., p. 75.
96. John Gorevan,' Elephant and Black Boy Tavern', 2002, *oldglasgowpubs.co.uk*: https://www.oldglasgowpubs.co.uk/blackboytavern.html#:~:text=The%20Black%20Boy%20Tavern%2C%20Gallowgate,forms%20part%20of%20the%20D
97. *Glasgow, Slavery and Atlantic Commerce*, p. 56.
98. 'Enslaved Black Boys', 28.3.2017, *Legacies of Slavery*: https://glasgowmuseumsslavery.co.uk/2017/03/28/enslaved-black-boys
99. Alan Greenlees, 'Glasgow and the campaign to end slavery', 5.10.2022, *Legacies of Slavery*: https://glasgowmuseumsslavery.co.uk/2022/10/05/glasgow-and-the-campaign-to-end-slavery/

100. David Armitage, 'An inhuman custom', 24-31.12.2021, *Times Literary Supplement*: https://www.the-tls.co.uk/articles/george-iii-slavery-archival-discovery-essay-david-armitage/
101. Dr Brooke Newman, 'Uncovering Royal Perspectives on Slavery, Empire, and the Rights of Colonial Subjects', *Georgian Papers Programme*: https://georgianpapers.com/2019/01/21/uncovering-royal-perspectives-on-slavery-empire-and-the-rights-of-colonial-subjects/
102. *Glasgow, Slavery and Atlantic Commerce*, p. 110.
103. Ibid., p. 100.
104. Ibid., p. 99.
105. Ibid., p. 101.
106. 'Germiston House', *TheGlasgowStory*: https://www.theglasgowstory.com/image/?inum=TGSB00277&t=2
107. *Glasgow, Slavery and Atlantic Commerce*, p. 39.
108. 'Glasgow, Germiston House, (Site Of)', *Canmore*: https://canmore.org.uk/site/171092/glasgow-germiston-house-site-of
109. *Glasgow, Slavery and Atlantic Commerce*, p.107
110. 'Gilmorehill House', *TheGlasgowStory*: https://www.theglasgowstory.com/image/?inum=TGSB00278
111. 'Gilmorehill House', *The University of Glasgow Story, University of Glasgow*: https://www.universitystory.gla.ac.uk/building/?id=131
112. Ian Marland, 'How this slaveowner's West End roots are being used to confront university's past', 23.8.2019, *Glasgow West End Today*: https://www.glasgowwestendtoday.scot/news/how-this-slaveowners-west-end-roots-are-being-used-to-confront-universitys-past-752/
113. Michael Taylor, 'Britain's role in slavery was not to end it, but to thwart abolition at every turn', 20.6.2020, *The Guardian*: https://www.theguardian.com/commentisfree/2020/jun/20/gladstone-wellington-peel-britain-pro-slavery-british-history-abolition
114. 'John Gladstone', *LBS database*, http://wwwdepts-live.ucl.ac.uk/lbs/person/view/8961
115. 'William Ewart Gladstone', *LBS database*: http://wwwdepts-live.ucl.ac.uk/lbs/person/view/2146630326
116. Jonathan Schofield, 'A closer look at some other plinth people: Heywood and Gladstone', 11.6.2020, *Confidentials: Manchester*: https://confidentials.com/manchester/heywood-and-gladstone-a-closer-look-at-some-other-plinth-people
117. 'Andrew Cochrane', *TheGlasgowStory*: https://www.theglasgowstory.com/image/?inum=TGSA02091
118. 'Cathedral', *It Wisnae Us*: https://it.wisnae.us/cathedral/
119. Brian Smith, 'The McDowalls', *PB The Cairn: Lochwinnoch Through the Ages*: https://www.pbthecairn.com/the-mcdowalls
120. Michael Moss, 'John Glassford of Dougalston', *TheGlasgowStory*: https://www.theglasgowstory.com/story/?id=TGSBH02
121. *Glasgow, Slavery and Atlantic Commerce*, p. 22.
122. 'Shawfield Mansion', *It Wisnae Us*: https://it.wisnae.us/shawfield-mansion
123. Sir Tom Devine, 'The Glassford Portrait', 28.9.2016, *How Glasgow Flourished* (Glasgow Museums): https://howglasgowflourished.wordpress.com/2016/09/28/the-glassford-portrait/
124. 'Shawfield Mansion', *It Wisnae Us*.
125. Anthony Lewis, 'The Shawfield Mansion', 21.10.2016, *How Glasgow Flourished* (Glasgow Museums): https://howglasgowflourished.wordpress.com/2016/10/21/the-shawfield-mansion-anthony-lewis/
126. Carol Foreman, 'The Shawfield Mansion', *Lost Glasgow*, Birlinn, 2019 (accessed via Google Books).
127. 'Golfhill House', 2008-23, *Dennistoun Conservation Society*: https://dennistounconservationsociety.org.uk/page/32.golfhill-house/#:~:text=The%20Estate%20known%20as%20Golfhill,merchant%20in%20Glasgow%2C%20in%201756.
128. 'Glasgow, Golfhill House', *Canmore*: https://canmore.org.uk/site/168503/glasgow-golfhill-house
129. 'James Dennistoun of Golfhill', *LBS database*: http://wwwdepts-live.ucl.ac.uk/lbs/person/view/2146646285
130. 'Golfhill', *Old Country Houses*: http://www.glasgowwestaddress.co.uk/Old_Country_Houses/Golfhill_House.htm
131. 'Alexander Dennistoun', *LBS database*: http://wwwdepts-live.ucl.ac.uk/lbs/person/view/2146002337
132. 'Bahamas 82', *LBS database*: http://wwwdepts-live.ucl.ac.uk/lbs/claim/view/2120002196
133. 'Alexander Dennistoun', 2022, *Wikipedia*: https://en.wikipedia.org/wiki/Alexander_Dennistoun, quoting "26. Alex Dennistoun" from *Memoirs and portraits of one hundred Glasgow men who have died during the last thirty years and in their lives did much to make the city what it now is* by James MacLehose (1886)
134. 'Archibald Graham Lang', *LBS database*: http://wwwdepts-live.ucl.ac.uk/lbs/person/view/46924
135. *Glasgow, Slavery and Atlantic Commerce*, p. 108.
136. 'Greenfield House', *TheGlasgowStory*: https://www.theglasgowstory.com/image/?inum=TGSB00282&t=2
137. *Glasgow, Slavery and Atlantic Commerce*, p. 111.

138. 'Greenview School, 47 Greenhead Street, Glasgow', 2010, *British Listed Buildings*: https://britishlistedbuildings.co.uk/200377898-greenview-school-47-greenhead-street-glasgow-glasgow#.Y8fhWOzP1Vc
139. 'James Buchanan of Moray Place', *LBS database*: http://wwwdepts-live.ucl.ac.uk/lbs/person/view/2146652835
140. *Glasgow, Slavery and Atlantic Commerce*, pp. 85-86.
141. 'Greenview School, 47 Greenhead Street, Glasgow', 2010, *British Listed Buildings*
142. *Glasgow, Slavery and Atlantic Commerce*, p. 108.
143. 'John Hamilton of Northpark', *LBS database*: http://wwwdepts-live.ucl.ac.uk/lbs/person/view/2146633009
144. 'Helen Hamilton (née Bogle)', *LBS database*: http://wwwdepts-live.ucl.ac.uk/lbs/person/view/2146633003.
145. 'George William Hamilton', *LBS database*: http://wwwdepts-live.ucl.ac.uk/lbs/person/view/14412
146. 'William Hamilton', *LBS database*: http://wwwdepts-live.ucl.ac.uk/lbs/person/view/45268.
147. 'John Hamilton of Northpark', *LBS database*: http://wwwdepts-live.ucl.ac.uk/lbs/person/view/2146633009
148. 'Robert Hamilton', *LBS database*: http://wwwdepts-live.ucl.ac.uk/lbs/person/view/46362
149. Dr Irene O'Brien, 'Amazing history of Glasgow building which was once BBC headquarters', 6.11.2022, *GlasgowTimes*: https://www.glasgowtimes.co.uk/news/23092736.amazing-history-glasgow-building-bbc-headquarters/
150. *Glasgow, Slavery and Atlantic Commerce*, p. 38.
151. Ibid., p.108.
152. Mark Harvey, 'Slavery, coerced labour and the development of industrial capitalism in Britain (4.10.19), *History Workshop*: https://www.historyworkshop.org.uk/empire-decolonisation/slavery-coerced-labour-and-the-development-of-industrial-capitalism-in-britain/
153. 'Henry Houldsworth', *TheGlasgowStory*, https://www.theglasgowstory.com/image/?inum=TGSA03590&add=99&t=0
154. 'Househill', *Old Country Houses*: http://www.glasgowwestaddress.co.uk/Old_Country_Houses/Househill.htm#ref4
155. 'Killearn House', *Killearn Heritage Trail*: https://killearnheritage.org.uk/killearn-house/
156. 'John Blackburn', *LBS database*: http://wwwdepts-live.ucl.ac.uk/lbs/person/view/20601
157. 'Househill (Hous'hill)', *TheGlasgowStory*: https://www.theglasgowstory.com/image/?inum=TGSB00285&t=2
158. 'Ingram Street', *TheGlasgowStory*: https://www.theglasgowstory.com/image/?inum=TGSA01053&t=2
159. 'Volume 3 – Chapter XXXIII – Manufactures and Manufacturers' (from *The History of Glasgow* by Robert Renwick and Sir John Lindsay, 1921, reproduced at *The History of Glasgow*: https://www.electricscotland.com/history/glasgow/glasgow3_33.htm
160. 'Archibald Ingram of St Kitts and St Vincent', *LBS database*: http://wwwdepts-live.ucl.ac.uk/lbs/person/view/2146654753.
161. 'Ottley Hall (St Vincent)', *LBS database*: http://wwwdepts-live.ucl.ac.uk/lbs/estate/view/3610.
162. 'Archibald Ingram', *TheGlasgowStory*: https://www.theglasgowstory.com/image/?inum=TGSE00950&t=2
163. 'Ramshorn Kirk', *It Wisnae Us*: https://it.wisnae.us/ramshorn-kirk/
164. 'Jamaica Street', *It Wisnae Us*: https://it.wisnae.us/jamaica-street/
165. *Glasgow, Slavery and Atlantic Commerce*, p. 30.
166. 'Alexander Houston or Houstoun the elder, of Jordanhill', *LBS database*: http://wwwdepts-live.ucl.ac.uk/lbs/person/view/2146654303.
167. 'Robert Houstoun', *LBS database*: http://wwwdepts-live.ucl.ac.uk/lbs/person/view/10480.
168. 'Jordanhill House', *TheGlasgowStory*, https://www.theglasgowstory.com/image/?inum=TGSB00287&t=2
169. 'Archibald Smith of Jordanhill', 'Leitch', 30.4.2022, *Geni*: https://www.geni.com/people/Archibald-Smith-of-Jordanhill/6000000024438528583
170. 'Archibald Smith of Jordanhill', *LBS database*: http://wwwdepts-live.ucl.ac.uk/lbs/person/view/2146646081.
171. 'James Smith of Jordanhill', *LBS database*: http://wwwdepts-live.ucl.ac.uk/lbs/person/view/10469.
172. 'Archibald Smith', *LBS database*: http://wwwdepts-live.ucl.ac.uk/lbs/person/view/42021.
173. 'William Smith of Carbeth Guthrie', *LBS database*: http://wwwdepts-live.ucl.ac.uk/lbs/person/view/28824.
174. 'Archibald Stirling the younger', *LBS database*: http://wwwdepts-live.ucl.ac.uk/lbs/person/view/18902.
175. 'Dictionary of National Biography, 1885-1900/Stirling-Maxwell, William' (14.11.21), *Wikisource*: https://en.wikisource.org/wiki/Dictionary_of_National_Biography,_1885-1900/Stirling-Maxwell,_William.
176. 'Kelvingrove House', *TheGlasgowStory*: https://www.theglasgowstory.com/image/?inum=TGSB00289&t=2.
177. 'Patrick Colquhoun', *The University of Glasgow Story*: https://www.universitystory.gla.ac.uk/biography/?id=WH0206&type=P.
178. 'Patrick Colquhoun', *LBS database*: http://wwwdepts-live.ucl.ac.uk/lbs/person/view/2146663865.

179. 'John Pattison', *TheGlasgowStory*: https://www.theglasgowstory.com/image/?inum=TGSA03583.
180. 'Richard Dennistoun d. 1833', *LBS database*: http://wwwdepts-live.ucl.ac.uk/lbs/person/view/44548.
181. 'Glasgow, Kelvingrove, Kelvingrove House', *Canmore*: https://canmore.org.uk/site/165101/glasgow-kelvingrove-kelvingrove-house.
182. 'Kelvingrove House', *TheGlasgowStory*.
183. *Glasgow, Slavery and Atlantic Commerce*, p. 109.
184. 'Kenmure House', *TheGlasgowStory*: https://www.theglasgowstory.com/image/?inum=TGSB00291#
185. *Glasgow, Slavery and Atlantic Commerce*, p. 87.
186. Ibid., pp. 76-77.
187. Ibid., p. 92.
188. Paula Dumas, 'Glasgow's West India Committee' (20.1.16), *Isles Abroad: A Group Blog of British and Irish Global History*: https://britishandirishhistory.wordpress.com/2016/01/20/glasgows-west-india-committee/
189. 'Aikenhead House', *TheGlasgowStory*: www.theglasgowstory.com/image/?inum=TGSB00229
190. *Glasgow, Slavery and Atlantic Commerce*, p. 110.
191. '19th century changes', *Linn Park et alia loca*: https://linnpark.tdocplus.co.uk/index.php/some-history/overview-of-lands/19th-century-changes
192. *Glasgow, Slavery and Atlantic Commerce*, p. 93.
193. 'Colin Campbell of Glasgow and Rotterdam', *LBS database*: http://wwwdepts-live.ucl.ac.uk/lbs/person/view/2146652289
194. Ibid.
195. 'Dalbeth', *Old Country Houses*: http://www.glasgowwestaddress.co.uk/Old_Country_Houses/Dalbeth.htm
196. 'Thomas HOPKIRK and Elizabeth SMELLIE' (18.6.11), *HOPKIRK FAMILY WORLDWIDE*: http://www.hopkirk.org/hopkirk/Page1223.html.
197. 'Dalbeth House': *TheGlasgowStory*: https://www.theglasgowstory.com/image/?inum=TGSB00260
198. T. M. Devine, 'An eighteen-century business elite: Glasgow-West India merchants, c. 1750-1815, *The Scottish Historical Review* Vol. 57, No. 163, Part 1 (Apr. 1978), p. 61.
199. 'Braidfauld', *Wikipedia*: https://en.wikipedia.org/wiki/Braidfauld#:~:text=The%20Church%20and%20school%20were,an%20extension%20to%20Dalbeth%20Cemetery.
200. *Glasgow, Slavery and Atlantic Commerce*, p. 59.
201. 'Alexander MacFarlane (1702-1755)', *Epsilon*, https://epsilon.ac.uk/view/epsilon-testbed/royal-society/nameregs/NA7222.
202. 'Alexander Macfarlane', *LBS database*: http://wwwdepts-live.ucl.ac.uk/lbs/person/view/2146644157.
203. *Glasgow, Slavery and Atlantic Commerce*, p. 111.
204. Ibid., p. 111.
205. Ibid., p. 8.
206. 'Petition to rename Glasgow street names which are named after slave owners', Change.org: https://www.change.org/p/glasgow-city-council-petition-to-rename-glasgow-street-names-which-are-named-after-slave-owners
207. 'A statement on Glasgow's Slavery Legacy from Council Leader Susan Aitken', Glasgow City Council: https://www.glasgow.gov.uk/index.aspx?articleid=27980
208. *Glasgow, Slavery and Atlantic Commerce*, p. 97.
209. 'Our Building', *Scottish Civic Trust*: https://www.scottishcivictrust.org.uk/our-building/
210. '140th anniversary of the founding of The Mitchell Library to be celebrated during National Libraries Week', 10.10.2017, *Glasgow Life*: https://www.glasgowlife.org.uk/news/140th-anniversary-of-the-founding-of-the-mitchell-library-to-be-celebrated-during-national-libraries-week
211. *Glasgow, Slavery and Atlantic Commerce*, pp. 89-90.
212. Ibid.
213. Ibid., p. 111.
214. Ibid., p. 100.
215. Ibid., p. 100.
216. Ibid., p. 80.
217. 'Saint Lucia History', 5.4.2023, *All About St Lucia*: https://allaboutstlucia.com/history/
218. Ibid.
219. *Glasgow, Slavery and Atlantic Commerce*, p. 112.
220. 'History of Saint Lucia', *Wikipedia*: https://en.wikipedia.org/wiki/History_of_Saint_Lucia
221. 'Saint Lucia History', 5.4.2023, *All About St Lucia*
222. 'Moore Park', *TheGlasgowStory*: https://www.theglasgowstory.com/image/?inum=TGSB00302&t=2
223. 'James Campbell of Moore Park', *LBS database*: http://wwwdepts-live.ucl.ac.uk/lbs/person/view/7250
224. 'Moorepark, Glasgow', 8.4.2022, *Wikipedia*: https://en.wikipedia.org/wiki/Moorepark,_Glasgow
225. 'Mount Vernon', *TheGlasgowStory*: https://www.theglasgowstory.com/image/?inum=TGSB00304&t=2
226. *Glasgow, Slavery and Atlantic Commerce*, p. 112.
227. Ibid., pp. 96-97.
228. 'Nelson Mandela', *TheGlasgowStory*: https://www.theglasgowstory.com/image/?inum=TGSA00948&t=2
229. *Glasgow, Slavery and Atlantic Commerce*, p. 102.
230. Ibid., pp.112-113.
231. Alan Cross, 'Nelson and the Slave Trade: A Position Statement by The Nelson Society', 15.6.2020, https://nelson-society.com/nelson-and-the-slave-trade-a-position-statement-by-the-nelson-society/

232. 'Northwoodside House', *Old Country Houses*: http://www.glasgowwestaddress.co.uk/Old_Country_Houses/Northwoodside_House.htm
233. Ibid.
234. 'Northwoodside House', *TheGlasgowStory*: https://www.theglasgowstory.com/image/?inum=TGSB00306&t=2
235. *Glasgow, Slavery and Atlantic Commerce*, p. 113.
236. Alistair McIntyre, 'The Oswalds of Gorton', 2013, *The Hidden Heritage of a Landscape*: https://hiddenheritage.org.uk/docs/060_308__oswaldsofgortanbyalistairmcintyre_1596991624.pdf
237. 'William Pitt on Abolition', Onview: Digital Collections & Exhibits, *Centre for the History of Medicine at County Library*: https://collections.countway.harvard.edu/onview/exhibits/show/this-abominable-traffic/william-pitt-abolition
238. *Glasgow, Slavery and Atlantic Commerce*, pp. 113-114.
239. 'Plantation House', *TheGlasgowStory*: https://www.theglasgowstory.com/image/?inum=TGSB00308&t=2
240. 'John Robertson of Plantation', *LBS database*: http://wwwdepts-live.ucl.ac.uk/lbs/person/view/44179
241. Prospect Estate [Grenada | Carriacou]', *LBS database*: http://wwwdepts-live.ucl.ac.uk/lbs/estate/view/10545
242. 'St Vincent 490A & B (Mount Pleasant)', *LBS database*: http://wwwdepts-live.ucl.ac.uk/lbs/claim/view/27264
243. *Glasgow, Slavery and Atlantic Commerce*, pp. 90-91.
244. Stuart Nisbet, 'Renfrewshire's Slave Legacy 5 The Maxwells of Pollok', 2019, *Renfrewshire Local History Forum*: https://rlhf.info/renfrewshires-slave-legacy-5-the-maxwells-of-pollok/
245. *Glasgow, Slavery and Atlantic Commerce*, pp. 90-91.
246. Ibid., p. 106.
247. 'Sir Lawrence Dundas 1st Bart.', *LBS database*: http://wwwdepts-live.ucl.ac.uk/lbs/person/view/2146656113
248. 'Dominica 576A & B (Castle Bruce)', *LBS database*: http://wwwdepts-live.ucl.ac.uk/lbs/claim/view/9862
249. 'Lawrence Dundas, 1st Earl of Zetland', *LBS database*: http://wwwdepts-live.ucl.ac.uk/lbs/person/view/11279
250. 'Sir Thomas Dundas 1st Baron Dundas', *LBS database*: http://wwwdepts-live.ucl.ac.uk/lbs/person/view/2146660919
251. Stephen Mullen, 'The Great Glasgow West India House of John Campbell, Senior, & Co.', *Recovering Scotland's Slavery Past – The Caribbean Connection*, ed. T.M. Devine, Edinburgh University Press, 2015, p. 138.
252. 'Alexander Campbell of Possil', *LBS database*: http://wwwdepts-live.ucl.ac.uk/lbs/person/view/10482
253. 'Mount Rose [Grenada | St Patrick]', *LBS database*: http://wwwdepts-live.ucl.ac.uk/lbs/estate/view/1292
254. 'Possil', *Old Country Houses*: http://www.glasgowwestaddress.co.uk/Old_Country_Houses/Possil.htm
255. 'Glasgow, Crawford Mansion', *Canmore*: https://canmore.org.uk/site/168448/glasgow-crawford-mansion
256. *Glasgow, Slavery and Atlantic Commerce*, p.115.
257. Ibid., pp. 114-115.
258. Alistair Mutch, 'Europe, the British Empire and the Madeira Trade: Catholicism, Commerce and the Gordon of Letterfourie Network c. 1730–c. 1800', 2016, *Northern Scotland*, Volume 7 Issue 1, Page 21-42: https://www.euppublishing.com/doi/abs/10.3366/nor.2016.0106?role=tab
259. 'History of Madeira', *Wikipedia*: https://en.wikipedia.org/wiki/History_of_Madeira
260. 'Madeira Island History', *São Pedro Association*: http://www.sanpedroassociation.com/shist.htm
261. *Glasgow, Slavery and Atlantic Commerce*, p. 95.
262. Ibid., p. 96.
263. Thomas Goldsmith, 'The Duke of Wellington and British Foreign Policy, 1814-1830', 2016, PHd thesis, University of East Anglia: https://core.ac.uk/download/pdf/196592261.pdf
264. *Hansard*, ABOLITION OF SLAVERY. HL Deb 17 May 1833 vol 17 1341: https://api.parliament.uk/historic-hansard/lords/1833/may/17/abolition-of-slavery#S3V0017P0_18330517_HOL_10
265. Dr Michael Taylor, 'Britain's role in slavery was not to end it, but to thwart abolition at every turn', 20.6.2020, *The Guardian*: https://www.theguardian.com/commentisfree/2020/jun/20/gladstone-wellington-peel-britain-pro-slavery-british-history-abolition#:~:text=And%20what%20of%20the%20Duke,behind%20the%20West%20India%20interest.
266. 'Ruchill', *Old Country Houses*: http://www.glasgowwestaddress.co.uk/Old_Country_Houses/Ruchill.htm
267. *Glasgow, Slavery and Atlantic Commerce*, p. 75.
268. Ibid.
269. 'Glasgow, Ruchill House', *Canmore*: https://canmore.org.uk/site/169555/glasgow-ruchill-house
270. 'Ruchill', *Old Country Houses*: http://www.glasgowwestaddress.co.uk/Old_Country_Houses/Ruchill.htm
271. 'Ruchill House', *TheGlasgowStory*: https://www.theglasgowstory.com/image/?inum=TGSB00314&t=2
272. 'St Andrews in the Square', *It Wisnae Us*: https://it.wisnae.us/st-andrews-in-the-square/

273. 'William Mathieson', *LBS database*: https://www.ucl.ac.uk/lbs/person/view/42850
274. *It Wisnae Us*: https://it.wisnae.us/glasgow-and-the-slave-trade/
275. Ibid.
276. Stuart McLean, 'The Oswalds of Scotstoun', 2005, *Jordanhill Local History*: http://www.wsmclean.com/Oswalds.htm
277. 'George Oswald of Scotstoun and Auchincruive', *The University of Glasgow Story*: https://www.universitystory.gla.ac.uk/biography/?id=WH0912&type=P
278. 'Scotstoun House', *TheGlasgowStory*: https://www.theglasgowstory.com/image/?inum=TGSB00315&t=2
279. *Glasgow, Slavery and Atlantic Commerce*, p.
280. 'Shield Hall', *Old Country Houses*: http://www.glasgowwestaddress.co.uk/Old_Country_Houses/Shield_Hall.htm#note2
281. 'Merchant Estates and Improvements', *It Wisnae Us*: https://it.wisnae.us/merchant-estates-and-improvements/
282. *Glasgow, Slavery and Atlantic Commerce*, p. 101.
283. 'Shield Hall', *TheGlasgowStory*: https://www.theglasgowstory.com/image/?inum=TGSB00317&t=2
284. *Glasgow, Slavery and Atlantic Commerce*, p. 115
285. 'North Speirs Wharf', *TheGlasgowStory*: https://www.theglasgowstory.com/image/?inum=TGSE00291
286. 'Glasgow, Springbank House', *Canmore*: https://canmore.org.uk/site/169038/glasgow-springbank-house
287. 'Springbank House', *TheGlasgowStory*: https://www.theglasgowstory.com/image/?inum=TGSB00319&t=2
288. 'Springbank House', *Old Country Houses*: http://www.glasgowwestaddress.co.uk/Old_Country_Houses/Springbank_House.htm
289. Stuart McLean, 'The Oswalds of Scotstoun', 2005, *Jordanhill Local History*: http://www.wsmclean.com/Oswalds.htm
290. 'Matthew Orr', *The Glasgow University Story*: https://universitystory.gla.ac.uk/biography/?id=WH25518&type=P
291. *Glasgow, Slavery and Atlantic Commerce*, p. 63.
292. Ibid.
293. 'Thomas Orr', *LBS database*: http://wwwdepts-live.ucl.ac.uk/lbs/person/view/2146632768
294. 'Matthew Orr', *LBS database*: s-live.ucl.ac.uk/lbs/person/view/2146632265
295. 'John Orr', *LBS database*: http://wwwdepts-live.ucl.ac.uk/lbs/person/view/2146632773
296. Ibid.
297. 'Thomas Orr of Tobago', *LBS database*: http://wwwdepts-live.ucl.ac.uk/lbs/person/view/2146633598
298. Ibid.
299. *Glasgow, Slavery and Atlantic Commerce*, p. 38.
300. 'Tontine on fire', *TheGlasgowStory*: https://www.theglasgowstory.com/image/?inum=TGSE00375&t=2
301. 'Tontine Rooms', *It Wisnae Us*: https://it.wisnae.us/tontine-rooms/
302. *Glasgow, Slavery and Atlantic Commerce*, p. 96.
303. 'Bonnie Prince Charlie and the Whistling' Kirk', 24.5.2019, *Lost Glasgow*: https://www.lostglasgow.scot/posts/bonnie-prince-charlie-and-the-whistlin-kirk-322/
304. *Glasgow, Slavery and Atlantic Commerce*, p. 96.
305. Stephen Mullen and Simon Newman, 'Slavery, Abolition and the University of Glasgow report and recommendations of the University of GlasgowHistory of Slavery Steering Committee', September 2018, University of Glasgow, p. 15: https://www.gla.ac.uk/media/Media_607547_smxx.pdf
306. 'Historical Slavery Initiative', *University of Glasgow*: https://www.gla.ac.uk/explore/historicalslaveryinitiative/uwi/
307. 'Anderson's College, Glasgow', University of Strathclyde Archives and Special Collections: https://atom.lib.strath.ac.uk/andersons-college-glasgow
308. Stephen Ramsay, 'Scotland's Dark History of Colonial Exploitation', 27.10.2021: https://medium.com/@stephenramsay_88358/scotlands-dark-history-of-colonial-exploitation-a6da43c25057
309. George Manzor, 'Alexander Speirs – Tobacco Lord (1714 – 1782) Part 2, 2020, *Glasgow's Benefactors*: https://glasgowbenefactors.com/2020/05/14/alexander-speirs-tobacco-lord-1714-1782-part-2/#_edn31
310. *It Wisnae Us*: https://it.wisnae.us/virginia-mansion/
311. 'Rosebank', *Old Country Houses*: http://www.glasgowwestaddress.co.uk/Old_Country_Houses/Rosebank.htm
312. 'About', *The Corinthian Club*: https://www.thecorinthianclub.co.uk/about/
313. *Glasgow, Slavery and Atlantic Commerce*, p. 104.
314. 'The Abolition of Slavery in the British Empire', *It Wisnae Us*: https://it.wisnae.us/the-abolition-of-slavery-in-the-british-empire/
315. 'The Fight for Universal Emancipation', *It Wisnae Us*: https://it.wisnae.us/the-fight-for-universal-emancipation/
316. 'Whitehill House', *TheGlasgowStory*: https://www.theglasgowstory.com/image/?inum=TGSB00326
317. 'Whitehill House', *Old Country Houses*: http://www.glasgowwestaddress.co.uk/Old_Country_Houses/Whitehill_House.htm
318. 'John Wallace', *TheGlasgowStory*: https://www.theglasgowstory.com/image/?inum=TGSA03544

319. George Manzor, 'Alexander Speirs – Tobacco Lord (1714 – 1782) Part 2', 2020, *Glasgow's Benefactors*: https://glasgowbenefactors.com/2020/05/14/alexander-speirs-tobacco-lord-1714-1782-part-2/
320. 'Yorkhill House', *Old Country Houses*: http://www.glasgowwestaddress.co.uk/Old_Country_Houses/Yorkhill_House.htm
321. 'Glasgow, Thornbank House', *Canmore*: https://canmore.org.uk/site/165152/glasgow-thornbank-house
322. *Glasgow, Slavery and Atlantic Commerce*, p. 84.
323. 'Yorkhill House', *TheGlasgowStory*: https://www.theglasgowstory.com/image/?inum=TGSB00328&t=2
324. 'Kilmardinny', *Old Country Houses*: http://www.glasgowwestaddress.co.uk/Old_Country_Houses/Kilmardinny.htm
325. *Glasgow, Slavery and Atlantic Commerce*, pp. 87-88.
326. 'Kilmardinny', *Old Country Houses*: http://www.glasgowwestaddress.co.uk/Old_Country_Houses/Kilmardinny.htm
327. 'William Brown of Kilmardinny', *LBS database*: http://wwwdepts-live.ucl.ac.uk/lbs/person/view/46881
328. 'About Us', Kilmardinny House: https://kilmardinnyhouse.co.uk/about-us/
329. 'Charles Stirling of Cadder', *LBS database*: http://wwwdepts-live.ucl.ac.uk/lbs/person/view/2146645829
330. 'Charles Stirling of Cadder', *LBS database*: http://wwwdepts-live.ucl.ac.uk/lbs/person/view/2146645829
331. Stuart Nisbet, 'Uncovering the History of Greenbank', 2010, Mearns History Group: https://www.mearnshistory.org.uk/index.php/history/mansion-houses/history-of-greenbank
332. 'Maitland Hutchinson or Hutchison or Hutcheson', *LBS database*: http://wwwdepts-live.ucl.ac.uk/lbs/person/view/2146651033
333. Stuart Nisbet, 'Netherlee, Williamwood House: Ground Survey', 2009, *Canmore*: https://canmore.org.uk/site/43822/netherlee-williamwood-house
334. 'James Finlay & Company', *LBS database*: https://www.ucl.ac.uk/lbs/firm/view/1296552023
335. 'Cambuslang, Rosebank House', *Canmore*: https://canmore.org.uk/site/203261/cambuslang-rosebank-house
336. 'Rosebank', *Old Country Houses* of the Old Glasgow Gentry: http://www.glasgowwestaddress.co.uk/Old_Country_Houses/Rosebank.htm
337. *Glasgow, Slavery and Atlantic Commerce*, p. 79.
338. 'Rosebank', *Old Country Houses* of the Old Glasgow Gentry: http://www.glasgowwestaddress.co.uk/Old_Country_Houses/Rosebank.htm
339. Ibid.
340. Iain Whyte, 'The Anti-Slave Trade Tour of William Dickson in 1792', *Scottish Local History*, Issue 72, Spring 2008.
341. 'The Campaign to Abolish the Slave Trade', *It Wisnae Us*: https://it.wisnae.us/the-campaign-to-abolish-the-slave-trade/
342. 'John Glassford', *Wikipedia*: https://en.wikipedia.org/wiki/John_Glassford
343. Thomas Nugent, 'Glassford House from the air', *Geograph*: https://www.geograph.org.uk/photo/6262921
344. 'Clober House', *TheGlasgowStory*: https://www.theglasgowstory.com/image/?inum=TGSB00251&t=2
345. 'Mains', *Old Country Houses*: http://www.glasgowwestaddress.co.uk/Old_Country_Houses/Mains.htm
346. Sandy Stevenson, *Tour Scotland*: 'Old Photograph Southfield House Newton Mearns Scotland': https://tour-scotland-photographs.blogspot.com/2015/08/old-photograph-southfield-house-newton.html
347. 'Maitland Hutchison', *LBS database*: https://www.ucl.ac.uk/lbs/person/view/2146651033
348. 'Southfield House, Mearns Hospital', *British Listed Buildings*: https://britishlistedbuildings.co.uk/200353522-southfield-house-mearns-hospital-mearns#.Y5yqKBCnwgo
349. *Glasgow, Slavery and Atlantic Commerce*, p. 46.
350. 'Shawfield', *Old Country Houses*: http://www.glasgowwestaddress.co.uk/Old_Country_Houses/Shawfield.htm

The south bank of the Clyde estuary: Inverclyde and Renfrewshire including Neilston

Craigends

Craigends estate

The houses of this residential area bordering Houston and Crosslee are built on the grounds of Craigends estate, once home to the Cunninghame family. Through marriage, in 1732 the family came into ownership of Grandvale estate, Westmoreland Parish, Jamaica. Members of the family went to Jamaica to oversee their business there. At the time of abolition of slavery the estate had 185 enslaved people (around 300 had been recorded in the 1770s) and William Cunninghame (1801-52), who had acquired a further plantation in the 1820s[351], was awarded over £3,278 by the Slave Compensation Commission for Grandvale alone[352] (no compensation was paid for the other one, Dunstaffnage in Westmoreland Parish, so it may have been wound up before abolition).[353] His brother, Alexander Cunninghame, went on to become a leading Scottish industrialist. In partnership with James Merry and Alexander Alison, they formed the company Merry and Cunninghame which owned coal mines and founded the Glengarnock Steelworks in Ayrshire. The original Craigends House was demolished and replaced by a second mansion in the mid to late 1800s; this was itself demolished in 1972.[354]

Finlaystone House.

Finlaystone

Finlaystone House

Robert Cunninghame Graham (1735-97) succeeded to Finlaystone estate in 1796, 26 years after his return from Jamaica where he was a 'slave-owner, landowner and planter, politician and public servant'.[355]

From around 1802 until his death in 1825, Finlaystone House was home to Archibald Campbell (b. 1753), of the Campbells of Inverawe. He was a partner of Greenock-based Caribbean merchant firm Anderson, Campbell & Co.[356] Apparently he won the life rent of Finlaystone from its owner, a descendant of Robert Cunninghame Graham, at cards.[357] He started his business life working with a Glasgow tobacco trader before moving into the sugar trade, becoming a 'highly prosperous West Indies merchant who became colonel of [the Greenock] Militia on his retirement'.[358]

Gourock

Gourock Coat of Arms

After Duncan Darroch bought the Barony of Gourock in 1784, he was awarded a coat of arms by the Court of the Lord Lyon. The arms feature a shield, the right half of which – in reference to Darroch's Caribbean connections – features the image of a black man holding a dagger, standing waist deep in the sea with a sailing ship flying a Saltire in the background. Adopted by the town in 1954, the arms have been displayed in various locations throughout the town. After thorough investigation of Inverclyde's links to slavery[359], and public consultation, in 2022 Inverclyde Council resolved to remove the arms from display.[360]

Gourock Park

Gourock Park – formerly known as Darroch Park – was the site of Gourock House, home to the Darroch family.[361] In 1784 the Barony of Gourock was bought by merchant Duncan Darroch (1740-1823) on his return from the Caribbean. It is probable that Darroch originated from the Gourock area as there is a story that as a boy he had vowed to buy the lands. The estate included Gourock House, which was possibly built in the early 1700s. It was given to the town in 1913 and eventually demolished in 1947.[362] Darroch's son inherited the estate; later a general in the British Army, he was illegitimately born in Jamaica to Mary Rowan, probably a 'free coloured' woman.[363] Duncan Darroch, his son, and other descendants are interred in the Darroch family vault in Gourock Park, all that remains of their property. Darroch Drive, Gourock, is named after the family.[364]

Gourock House.

Kirn Drive

This was the site of Kempock House which in the 1840s was the home of Archibald Graham Lang (sometimes spelled Laing) (1801-75), partner in the Glasgow-based Caribbean trading company Gray, Roxburgh & Co.[365] (sometime Wighton, Gray & Co.). His co-partners were fellow Scots William Gray, James Thomas Brown and Thomas Roxburgh and all shared in Slave Compensation Commission awards totalling over £1,854 for two sugar plantations the company owned in Trinidad, one of which was called Friendship.[366] Together, these enslaved 35 people at the time of abolition. Kempock House was demolished in 2008.[367]

Greenock

Antigua Street / Jamaica Street / Jamaica Lane / Madeira Street / Tobago Street / Togo Place

Most of these were named after places where Greenock and West of Scotland merchants and landowners owned plantations which enslaved African people[368]; Togo Place is unusual as a direct reference to the West African 'slave coast' where people were taken into slavery by European slave traders.[369] Until 1775 many Greenock streets were unnamed, but with the development of the town that year the council deemed it 'necessary that the streets have names to distinguish them'.[370] The names chosen honoured leaders of the time, local landowners and the town's trading connections. In Madeira slavery was abolished in 1767, decades before Britain followed suit. The town's links to the Caribbean have been perpetuated into very recent times by the naming of the developments Jamaica Court and Jamaica Apartments.

Togo Place.

Ardgowan Street / Ardgowan Road / Ardgowan Place

Named after the Ardgowan estate, Inverkip, of the Shaw Stewart family.

Baker Street

Site of a sugar refinery built in 1831 by Alex. & Thos. Anderson; it burned down in 1851.[371] There were a number of sugar refineries in Greenock in the nineteenth century, some of which were established before the abolition of slavery in the British Empire.

Bentinck Street

William Henry Cavendish Bentinck, 3rd Duke of Portland (1738-1809), was twice Prime Minister of Britain, in 1783 and 1807-09.[372] As a politician he generally upheld the interests of slave-owning colonialists in the Caribbean and, during his first term as Prime Minister, did not reply to a letter from Granville Sharpe, one of the first to campaign against the slave trade. Sharp wrote to him in connection with the *Zong* slave ship case to argue against the 'monstrous injustice and abandoned wickedness' of the trade.[373] During its 'middle passage' voyage, the crew of the *Zong* murdered over 130 African people, including women and children, by throwing them overboard, supposedly to save drinking water; a number of captives chose to jump into the sea rather than allow themselves to be thrown in. In total 142 died and none of the crew was ever prosecuted.[374]

Bogle Street

Glasgow-based Caribbean merchant Robert Bogle (1757-1821) married into the Shaw Stewart family of Ardgowan, Inverkip. The street was the site of a sugar refinery – Greenock's third – built by Robert Macfie & Sons in 1802 and in use until 1854.[375]

Cappielow

This was the name – now given to Greenock Morton F.C.'s stadium – of the sugar refinery of Speirs & Wrede which opened in 1833 and operated until 1877.[376] After a fire around 1845, it was rebuilt.

Cathcart Street

According to the *Greenock Directory 1815-16*, No. 96 Cathcart Street was listed as the address of Agnew Crawford (d. 1834), merchant. He was definitely connected to the slave economy as a trustee and executor of the estate of Alexander Campbell[377] (d. 1826), owner of Jamaican plantations including Robin's Hall, Manchester. Possibly related to Crawford's mother, whose maiden name was Campbell, Campbell also left legacies to Agnew's two sisters, Arrabella and Marion Crawford. Agnew shared in a Slave Compensation Commission award of over £930 for Robin's Hall where 44 people were enslaved.[378] His sisters also submitted claims for this plantation but were unsuccessful. They lived in Mansion House (see *Greenock: Well Park*). Cathcart Street is also the site of a pub called The James Watt, named after the engineer who was connected to the slave trade.

Clarence Street

Site of the sugar refinery of William Leitch, after whom the town's Leitch Street is likely named. This opened in 1812[379] and burned down in 1847.[380]

Custom House Quay / Custom House Way

Custom House Quay is the site of the Custom House, designed by William Burn and completed in 1818.[381] The extent and grandeur of the building represented Greenock's trade success, much of it coming from the Caribbean. The building served as a meeting place for local merchants and was where duties on exports and imports at the port were paid. It remained in use by HM Revenue and Customs until 2010 and is now offices.[382]

Custom House Quay, Greenock, 1878.

East Crawford Street

Possibly named after the Crawford merchant family.[383]

East Shaw Street

Named after the Shaw Stewart family of Ardgowan estate, Inverkip.[384]

Fairrie Street

The sugar refinery of James Fairrie (1754-1815) was built at Cartsdyke Bridge in 1799 and Fairrie Street is probably named after him.[385] Fairrie was born in Irvine to shipmaster and Caribbean merchant James Farrie (different spelling) and became captain of one of the family's trading ships that sailed between Greenock and the Caribbean (he lost his arm on one voyage after the ship was captured by Spaniards). In 1797 he bought the Cartsdyke Bridge site and began to develop his sugar refining business.[386]

James Watt Building / James Watt Dock / James Watt Way / Watt Institution / Watt Library / Watt Street / The Watt Cairn (Greenock Cemetery)

James Watt (1736-1819) was the mechanical engineer whose design of steam engine, patented in 1769, was key to the development of the Industrial Revolution. Greenock-born, a number of the town's streets and institutions are named after him.[387] His father, James Watt (1698-1782), was a Greenock ship owner and merchant who did business with North Carolina and the Caribbean and who was known to have traded enslaved people. Watt Junior became his father's tobacco agent in Glasgow in the 1750s and trafficked an African child called Frederick to the Brodie family of Spynie, Moray.[388] The steam engine that he designed was in use in the Caribbean from the very early nineteenth century, contributing to the slavery-based economy in the milling of sugar

The Watt Institution.

cane and creating sugar syrup.³⁸⁹ In Cathcart Street there is a pub called The James Watt. The engineer is widely commemorated throughout Britain – for example in Glasgow's George Square and Nelson Mandela Place – and the unit of power was named after him in 1908. From the 1790s Watt privately supported the gradual abolition of plantation-based slavery.³⁹⁰

Johnston Street

The house Bellevue at No. 8 Johnston Street was the home of John Mcfarquhar, described as 'something of a Demerary' and owner of Johanna plantation in what is now Guyana. In 1832 this had 125 enslaved people. To pay off a debt, in 1836 Mcfarquhar's compensation of over £6,350 for this estate was paid to the partners of Glasgow-based Caribbean merchants John Campbell Senior & Co.³⁹¹

Bellevue House.

Ker Street

The derelict sugar refinery on this street marks the site where one was established in 1831³⁹² by Thomas Young & Co. The extant building was erected in the late-nineteenth century and became home to the Glebe Sugar Refinery Co., managed by Abram Lyle, a founder of Tate & Lyle.³⁹³

Leitch Street

This may have been named to recognise William Leitch[394] whose sugar refinery was in Clarence Street.

Nicolson Street

Probably named after Michael Stewart Nicholson[395], who took the name Shaw Stewart when he inherited Ardgowan estate, Inverkip, in 1812.[396]

Patrick Street

After abolition of slavery in British territories in 1833, anti-slavery campaigners kept up the fight to have slavery abolished in other countries and to stop Britain trading with other slave-based economies, particularly the United States. Abolitionists continued to tour the country and a number came to Greenock to speak. Best known among them was Frederick Douglass (1817-95), who appeared at the church on this street, near the junction with Grey Place. Douglass returned in 1860 and spoke at the Town Hall. Other campaigners who came to the town included former slaves Olaudah Equiano, Josiah Henson, Samuel Ringgold Ward and Macgregor Laird.[397]

Seafield Cottage Lane

Seafield Cottage, on Seafield Cottage Lane facing the Esplanade, was the retirement home of Jamaican plantation owner Robert Wallace (1773-1855), son of Caribbean merchant and plantation owner John Wallace of Kelly estate, Wemyss Bay. Robert

Bellevue House.

was an MP for Greenock and a business partner of James Tasker (after whom Greenock's Tasker Street is named). After the depreciation in value of his Jamaican properties, a public subscription for him was raised, creating an annuity of £500 – this in spite of substantial compensation for the loss of enslaved labourers in Jamaica and the sale of Kelly estate.[398] He died at Seafield Cottage and his elaborate memorial and grave is in Greenock Cemetery; the inscription commemorates his campaigning for post office reform, including the introduction of penny postage.[399]

Roxburgh Street

The Roxburgh Plantation on Tobago was owned by the Shaw Stewart family of Ardgowan. This was the site of the Roxburgh Street Refinery, built to process sugar imports by the firm of Hugh Hutton & Co.[400]

Demolition of Roxburgh Street Refinery chimney

Sir Michael Street

This was named after Sir Michael Shaw Stewart (1788-1836), 6th Baronet of Ardgowan.[401]

Sugarhouse Lane

Now lost under the Oak Mall shopping centre, this was the site of Greenock's first sugar refinery, built in 1765 to process the burgeoning importations of raw sugar harvested by enslaved labourers on Caribbean plantations. It burned down in 1882. In 1788 a second refinery was built on the lane – this was twice burned down and rebuilt before final closure in 1886. Sugar refining was a key Greenock industry for over 200 years. Abram Lyle (1820-91), a founder of Tate & Lyle, was born in Greenock and operated the Glebe Sugar Refinery on Ker Street. Tate & Lyle ended sugar production in the town in 1997.[402] A number of other sugar refineries were built in Greenock throughout the nineteenth century, many after the abolition of slavery, so are not included here. However, the sugar industry was dependent on Caribbean slave labour for well over a century.

Tasker Street

James Tasker (1783-1867) was a Greenock merchant and his son, Patrick Tasker (1823-60), a merchant in Canada. With Robert Wallace of Seafield Cottage, James was partner in the firm Wallace Hunter. Both shared in Slave Compensation Awards of over £7,025 through financial connections to three Jamaican plantations: Saltspring Pen, St Elizabeth Parish; Spring Garden, Trelawney Parish; and Glenbirnie, Westmoreland Parish. Tasker was an investor in the Glasgow, Paisley and Greenock Railway and also a partner in the Greenock Brewery.[403]

Union Street

No. 40 was home to merchant James Tasker.[404]

Virginia Street

Named for the area of America where many West of Scotland merchants and landowners either owned or traded with tobacco plantations that used enslaved labour.[405]

Wallace Street / Wallace Place

These may be named after Robert Wallace (see *Seafield Cottage Lane*).[406]

Well Park

This land was formerly in the ownership of the Shaw family who built the early seventeenth-century Mansion House which stood in the area of the land which is now between present day Lynedoch Street and Terrace Road. On the death of the last of the Shaw line in 1752, the land and property passed to Sir John Stewart (1739-1812) who adopted the name Shaw Stewart. Mansion House was latterly let to tenants and demolished in 1886. All that remains of the original Shaw property is the elaborate well which carries a date stone of 1629.[407]

West Shaw Street

Again after the Shaw Stewart family of Ardgowan estate, Inverkip.

West Stewart Street

Also named after the Shaw Stewart family of Ardgowan estate.

Other Greenock connections to slavery

- In 1836 Greenock-born Elizabeth Martin and her son John, a merchant in the town and probably also a sugar refiner, claimed compensation for the Jamaican plantations of The Deanery and Long Bay, both of St Catherine Parish. Together these enslaved 144 people. The Martins inherited the plantations from unnamed relatives. Elizabeth Martin received compensation of over £2,653.[408]
- In the early nineteenth century Arthur Oughterson[409], a Greenock merchant, was owner of Brighton plantation, St George Parish, Barbados. A later owner claimed over £2,716 in compensation for the 128 people enslaved there.[410]
- Dugald Malcolm Ruthven[411] (d. 1815) was a merchant and partner in the Greenock Caribbean trading firm of Campbell, Ruthven and Lindsay, which went bust around 1804, leaving Ruthven bankrupt. His children were born in Jamaica and went on to co-own a plantation there.[412]
- Greenock has been said to be the birthplace of William – 'Captain' – Kidd, a Scottish privateer who was denounced as a pirate and had links to the tobacco and sugar trade. However, he himself claimed Dundee as his birthplace.
- Greenock was the arrival point for an African boy, originally called Aina, who was kidnapped by his own countrymen and sold into slavery, endured the 'middle passage', and after some time as a slave in Jamaica, was eventually sold to a Mr McColl, who brought him to Scotland. On arrival at Greenock McColl abandoned the boy who eventually made his way to Glasgow and then Edinburgh, at some point acquiring the name of George Dale. His brief account of his journey and experience – which, in particular, gives vivid insight into the horrors of the 'middle passage' – was given in 1790 when he was around 30 years old.[413]
- Greenock was a major exporter of salted herring which was sent to the Caribbean to feed enslaved people there.[414]

Houston House.

Houston

Houston estate

From around the 1720s, the estate of Houston was owned by Sir James Campbell (d. 1731), owner of sugar and rum-producing Grandvale estate in Westmoreland Parish, Jamaica, which had 921 enslaved people in 1737.[415] Houston estate was subsequently bought by another Caribbean merchant, Archibald Speirs, son of Alexander Speirs of Elderslie, who – using funds earned through slavery – built the planned village of Houston in the 1780s. He also built the present Houston House[416] (further alterations to this were carried out in the nineteenth century). James Campbell's sister, Margaret (d. 1754), married Alexander Porterfield of Duchal House, Kilmacolm, thus allowing yet another landowning family to share in the profits of slavery.

Inchinnan

Southbar

This house and estate, west of modern Inchinnan, was in the ownership of the Alexander family from the late eighteenth century and by the 1820s was occupied by William Maxwell Alexander (1790-1853) who, along with his brothers Boyd and Claud and a number of other men, was partner in the Caribbean trading firm Wm Fraser, Alexander, Neilson & Co. Through this association he shared in the award of over £41,918, paid on abolition for the loss of 1,765 enslaved people on nine plantations in Antigua, Grenada and St Vincent.[417] Southbar House was destroyed by fire in 1827 and rebuilt sometime after 1836 (most of the money from the Slave Compensation Commission was paid out to the beneficiaries that year). The house was burned to a ruin again in 1920 and demolished around 1950, though a farm steading converted to dwellings remains.[418]

Inverkip

Ardgowan Estate

North of Inverkip, the Ardgowan estate has been in the possession of the Stewart family (later the Shaw Stewarts) since the 1400s. The house was built between 1797 and 1801 for Sir John Shaw Stewart (1739-1812), 4th Baronet. He married the widow of Sir James Maxwell of Pollok, Glasgow, who was also the daughter of Robert Colhoun (or Colquhoun) of St Kitts. John was MP for Renfrewshire twice and was owner of Roxburgh estate in St Paul, Tobago.[419] He had inherited this from his father, Sir Michael Stewart (3rd Baronet, d. 1796) who had been given the estate by his brother, Archibald Stewart (d. 1779). Archibald bought land that would become Roxburgh in 1770 and 'released' the plantation to his brother in 1775; he was likely to have been a business partner of John Paul Jones, 'father of the US Navy', and was killed by American 'privateers' on Tobago four years later.[420]

Ardgowan House.

After Sir John, Roxburgh passed down to his nephew, Sir Michael Shaw Stewart (1766-1825), 5th Baronet, who gave it to his son, Admiral Sir Houston Stewart (1791-1875), who ultimately received over £2,998 in compensation for the 143 people enslaved at Roxburgh (on his death he was worth over £53,664[421]). The 5th Baronet's other sons were also connected to the slavery-based economy: Patrick Maxwell Stewart (1795-1846) was a London merchant and an agent in Tobago, and shared in Slave Compensation Commission awards of over £4,586 for links to two further Tobago plantations of Charlotteville and Observatory, which together were enslaving 220 people at the time of abolition (he made extensive investments in new railway companies that were springing up across Scotland); Sir Michael Shaw Stewart (1788-1836), 6th Baronet and MP for Lanarkshire and Renfrewshire successively, was married to the daughter of Robert Farquhar of Newark Castle, Port Glasgow, and inherited plantations on Trinidad and Tobago. As MP he campaigned for west of Scotland planters and merchants to receive compensation for the loss of their workforce on abolition.[422]

Members of the family from that era are buried in the Shaw Stewart Mausoleum in Inverkip Cemetery. Ardgowan House and estate is now run as a wedding and events venue.

Johnstone

Milliken estate

Lying north-west of Johnstone and south of Brookfield is farmland that was the Lands of Johnstone until 1729, when they were acquired by plantation owner James Milliken (1669-1741) on his return from around 36 years spent on the Caribbean islands of St

Kitts and Nevis. He demolished the old Johnstone Castle and built Milliken House in its place around 1733.[423] This burned down in 1801 and was replaced by another Milliken House (on a different site) in 1836, itself demolished in the 1930s.[424]

Ayrshire-born Milliken first owned a plantation on Nevis (112 enslaved people were recorded at this plantation in 1707) and then owned the Monkey Hill plantation on St Kitts where his friend William McDowall I of Castle Semple, Lochwinnoch, also owned plantations. He co-owned a slave ship with McDowall that sank on its maiden voyage, drowning 272 African people, and was co-partner with McDowall in Glasgow's South Sugar House.[425] His property in the Caribbean and Scotland passed down and enriched the succeeding generations of his family. Money from these business interests was also spent locally on agricultural improvements and the church.[426]

His son, James (1710-1776), was born in Nevis and after schooling in England went to St Kitts to run family affairs after his father returned to Scotland; he later became Rector of Glasgow University.[427] In 1834 his great-great-grandson Sir William Milliken Napier (1788-1852) was awarded £2,555 in compensation for the 161 people enslaved at Monkey Hill.[428]

Miliken House.

Kilmacolm

Duchal House

Lying south-west of Kilmacolm, this mansion was built in 1710 by Alexander Porterfield (1673-1743), whose family had owned the surrounding estate since the

Duchal House.

sixteenth century. Through marriage to Margaret Campbell of Craigends, in 1735 Porterfield inherited a share in the Grandvale estate, Westmoreland Parish, Jamaica, and this in turn passed to his grandson, Boyd Porterfield[429] (d. 1795), who sold his share around twenty years later. Grandvale produced sugar, rum, molasses, coffee and pimento.

Springbank House

In 1836 this was listed as the home of Alexander Ferrier, part-owner of a plantation in Surinam[430], now Suriname, who also built Bloomhill House in Cardross. This may also be the house noted as the marriage place of Andrew Scott to Celia King[431], daughter of Daniel King[432], a merchant of Port Glasgow, resident of Tobago, and likely owner of a plantation there, Sherwood Park in St Andrew Parish. One hundred and six people were enslaved there at the time of abolition; in 1836 Celia and her husband shared in a compensation award for the estate of over £2,070.[433]

Lochwinnoch

Castle Semple

This was purchased by Colonel William McDowall (1678-1748) in 1727. The McDowalls originated from Garthland, Galloway, and William arrived on the island of Nevis around 1695, becoming a plantation overseer. He then went to St Kitts and purchased enslaved people and plantations; he was also made 'colonel' in the island's militia. Returning to Britain 1724, he eventually settled in Glasgow and, along with his friend James Milliken of Milliken estate, Johnstone, he helped to significantly expand Glasgow's sugar trade. His wealth allowed him to purchase not only Castle Semple estate (building a new 31-room house), but also Shawfield Mansion in Glasgow, which he owned until selling it to John Glassford in the 1760s. In 1726 a ship he had purchased to transport enslaved African people overturned on its maiden journey – 272 African people died.[434] He brought many Africans back to Scotland, including one enslaved boy as his servant; his wife objected to this boy but McDowall threatened to leave her so she had to acquiesce to his presence![435]

William McDowall II (1719-84), inherited his father's estates and business properties; he was MP for Renfrewshire and partner in Caribbean trading firm Alexander Houston & Co.[436]. William II's sons carried on the Caribbean connections: David McDowall Grant (d. 1841) went to Jamaica; William McDowall III (1749-1810) became partner in Houston & Co., Rector of Glasgow University, Lord Lieutenant of Renfrewshire and MP at different times for Ayrshire, Renfrewshire and Glasgow Burghs (he is commemorated in Paisley Abbey); James McDowall was a Lord Provost of Glasgow who later died in St Lucia; Day Hort McDowall financed the building of Walkinshaw House[437], north of Paisley; and Laurence McDowall managed the family plantations on Grenada. In 1835, compensation for over £5,139 went to William III's nephew, William McDowall (1770-1840), for the 197 people enslaved[438] on the Grenada McDowall-owned estate, Mount Alexander. Before this he had to sell the family's Garthland estate at Lochwinnoch (known as Barr House before the McDowalls owned it) and then Castle Semple; much of the McDowalls' business concerns were part of Alexander Houston and Co., which had collapsed in 1795, leaving the family's wealth much reduced.

John Harvey (né Rae; d. 1820) purchased Castle Semple as a home for his retirement. He was a Grenada plantation owner and nephew of Robert Harvey of Aberdeenshire whose plantations on Grenada and Antigua enslaved over 1,000 people. On his death, Castle Semple passed to his daughter Margaret and her husband, James

Castle Semple House.

Lee. John Harvey had been owner and joint-owner of five estates on Grenada, holding a total of 869 enslaved people at the time of his death; compensation for two of these estates – totalling over £8,462 – was awarded to Margaret and James on abolition.[439] The Harvey family sold Castle Semple as a result of gambling debts in 1908 and the house was ruined by fire in 1924. It was demolished in the 1970s though four pavilions remain and have been converted into dwellings.[440]

Neilston

Neilstonside

The lands of Neilstonside, south-west of Neilston, were once owned by Caribbean merchant John Wallace of Kelly estate, Wemyss Bay.[441]

Paisley

Blackhall Manor

This sixteenth-century house, the oldest in Paisley, was owned by the Stewart family (later the Shaw Stewarts of Ardgowan estate, Inverkip) until they gifted it to the town in 1940.[442]

Blackhall Manor c. 1950. The manor was deroofed in the 1840s to save on taxes and by 1978 was in such poor condition that demolition was recommended. The plans were shelved after local outcry and in 1982-83 the manor was carefully restored and is once again a house.

Paisley Abbey

The Abbey features an elaborate memorial plaque to politician, Caribbean trader and plantation owner William McDowall III of Castle Semple, Lochwinnoch (b. 1749). Dated 1810, the year of his death, this was 'erected by the county ... in esteem for his private virtues and of gratitude for his public services'.

McDowall III Memorial.

Ralston

In 1755 this estate was purchased from the Duke of Hamilton by the Caribbean merchant and MP William McDowall II (1719-84).[443] His son, William III, who is commemorated in Paisley Abbey, sold the estate in 1800.

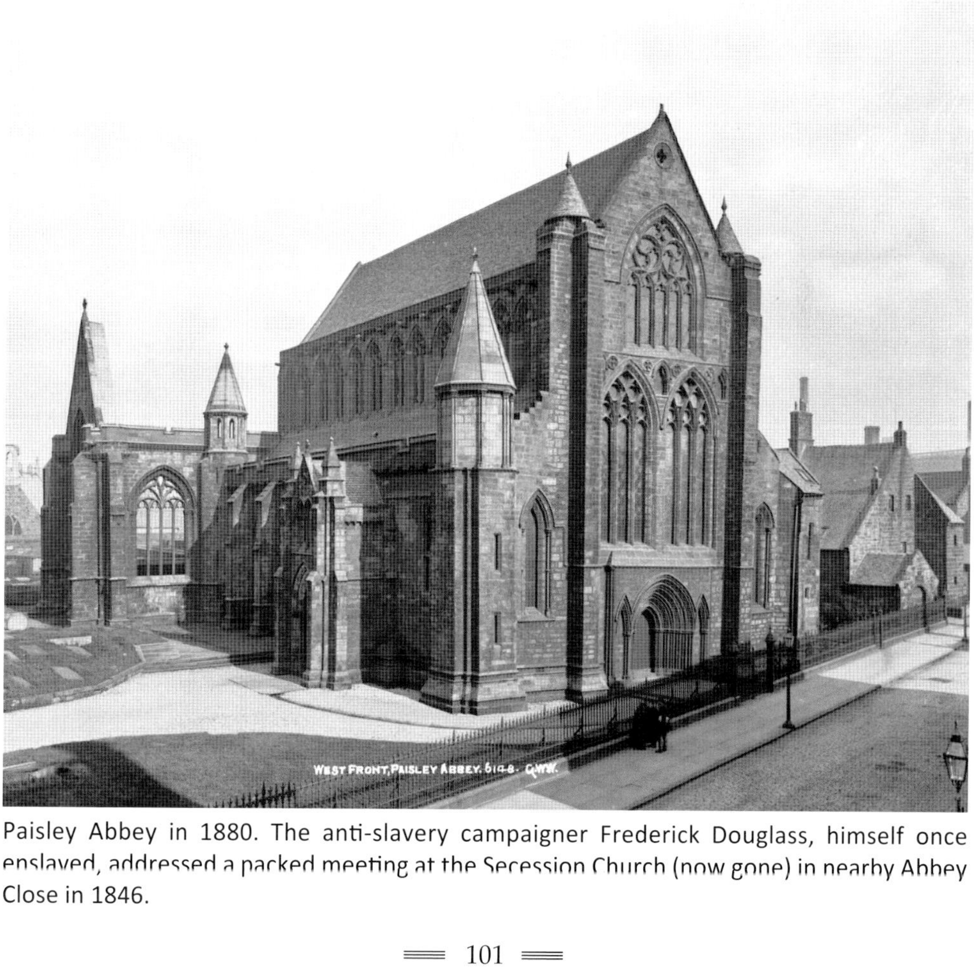

Paisley Abbey in 1880. The anti-slavery campaigner Frederick Douglass, himself once enslaved, addressed a packed meeting at the Secession Church (now gone) in nearby Abbey Close in 1846.

Port Glasgow

Bay Street

The Gourock Ropeworks building was previously the Birkmyre Mills, the 1886-built ropeworks of the Gourock Rope Company which was formed from a merger with the Port Glasgow Rope and Duck Company started by tobacco merchants. The mills ceased operation in 1976 and the building was later converted into flats.

Birkmyre Rope Works.

Farquhar Road

Probably named for Robert Farquhar of Newark Castle.[444]

Montgomerie Street

This commemorates Peter Montgomerie[445] (d. 1849), a Caribbean merchant of Port Glasgow who had previously lived on the island of St Croix.[446] His Port Glasgow home was the estate of Clune Park, the name later given to an area of shipyard workers' homes, now largely derelict. He was probably the nephew of Robert Montgomerie[447], also of Saint Croix (and later of Irvine, Ayrshire), and received a share of his sugar-producing Sevilla estate, Couva, Trinidad, on his death. Peter Montgomerie then shared in the compensation award of over £7,173 for this estate. In 1836, 160 people were recorded as enslaved there; the number had been as high as 218 in 1813.[448]

Newark Castle.

Newark Castle

From around 1820 this was owned by Robert Farquhar (1755-1836). He was the nephew of Robert Harvey, owner of plantations on Antigua and Grenada that enslaved over 1,000 people, and half-brother of John Harvey of Castle Semple, Lochwinnoch. Farquhar inherited an Antiguan estate belonging to Robert and three Grenadian estates belonging to John. Combined, these estates enslaved 900 people at the time of abolition and in 1835 Farquhar received over £17,930 in compensation.[449] After his death the castle and estate passed to his daughter Eliza, who retained ownership of the Caribbean estates. Her husband was Sir Michael Shaw Stewart of Ardgowan estate, Inverkip. The castle fell into disrepair as the nineteenth century continued and a later Shaw Stewart placed it in state care in 1909, after which it was restored.[450]

New Parish Church

Formerly St Andrew's Church, this 1823 kirk is built in the surrounds of an older cemetery which contains the gravestones of Caribbean and Virginia merchant and slave trader, Robert Allason (spelled Allison on the memorial stone), of Greenbank House, Clarkston, and his brother John, who worked as his agent in America along with a third brother William.[451]

Princes Street

Princes Street was the site of the mills and ropewalk of the Port Glasgow Rope and Duck Company.[452] This was started in 1736 in response to the rise of trade shipping from the port and the consequent demand for ropes and sailcloth. The original partners had vested interests in shipping: tobacco merchant Lawrence Dinwiddie and merchant and slave-trader Richard Oswald[453], of Germiston and Scotstoun, Glasgow, respectively. In 1797 the company merged with the Gourock Rope Company, established in Gourock's Cove Road in 1777, and continued under that name, eventually moving to the building now known as the Gourock Ropeworks on Bay Street in 1886. This had previously been a sugar refinery and became known as Birkmyre Mills after the family that became owners of the company.

Wallace Street

This may be named after Robert Wallace of Seafield Cottage, Greenock.[454]

Other Port Glasgow connections to slavery

- Alexander Fairley Harrower (d. 1842) was a merchant based in Port Glasgow, where he died.[455] In 1836 he was awarded compensation of £4,683 for three unnamed plantations in British Guiana. Together these enslaved 80 people.
- In 1756 Port Glasgow was the port of departure for Jamie Montgomery, enslaved by a landowner in Beith, Ayrshire, and trained as a joiner so that he could be sent to Virginia and sold for a profit due to his skills.[456] However, Montgomery escaped to Edinburgh where he was caught and imprisoned in the Tollbooth while his owner took legal action to recover his 'property'. In 1757 Montgomery died in prison before the case was heard.
- Port Glasgow was the landing place of all the cotton, sugar, rum, tobacco and other products of the slavery-based economy produced in America and the Caribbean.

Renfrew

King's Inch / Elderslie House

This Robert Adam-designed house, originally known as King's Inch and standing in the area of modern Renfrew bounded by Kenley Road, Crofton Square and Crofton Street[457], was completed in 1782 for Glasgow tobacco lord Alexander Speirs (1714-82). Edinburgh-born Speirs's wealth was estimated at about £153,000 (equivalent to around £273 million in relative income value in 2023). He bought the estate on which the house was built in 1767, from Helen Wallace, reputedly a descendant of William Wallace (Speirs owned broadswords that supposedly belonged to Wallace[458]).

He probably first went to Virginia as a plantation overseer in the 1730s and, through marriage to the daughter of a Virginian plantation owner, inherited land in Chesterfield County. With his wife (who died shortly after), he returned to Glasgow in 1750 and began to establish his business in importing tobacco, going into partnership with Archibald Buchanan (brother of Andrew, after whom Glasgow's Buchanan Street is named), amongst others; his second wife was Archibald Buchanan's

Elderslie House.

daughter. He was involved in civic life as treasurer of the city and served as a bailie. He also contributed money to the building of St Andrews by the Green Church in Turnbull Street, Glasgow.[459]

Between the mid-1750s and the start of the American Revolutionary War in 1775, he made vast sums from the tobacco trade which he invested in the development of his land and property (see *Glasgow: Ingram Street* and *Virginia Street*) and into other businesses (see *Glasgow: Candleriggs*). Managing to avoid some of the losses caused by the American war, from 1779 Speirs went into the Caribbean trades in tobacco, sugar, rum and coffee. On his death his personal wealth was £123,236, £46,510 due to him from interests in Virginia and Maryland. This money benefited his children and further generations well into the nineteenth century.

Speirs was also owner of the estates of Yoker, Blawarthill, Culcreuch and Houston.[460] He is commemorated on a stained-glass window in Glasgow Cathedral. Elderslie House was demolished in 1920.[461]

Blythswood

This area of Renfrew is named after the estate which once stretched from here to Glasgow. This was actually a combination of the original Ranfield (or Renfield) estate in Renfrew and that of Blythswood in Glasgow, both of which came into the ownership of the Campbell family.[462] In 1821 Blythswood House was built for Glasgow MP

Blythswood House.

Archibald Campbell (c. 1763-1838).[463] Campbell represented the interests of members of the Glasgow West India Association in Parliament.[464]

Wemyss Bay

Kelly Estate

Kelly House was built in 1793 and owned by John Wallace (1712-1805). As a partner in the trading firm of Somerville, Gordon and Co. (along with Charles Stirling of Cadder and John Gordon of Aikenhead amongst others), he made his fortune from trading in the Caribbean and owned three Jamaican estates: Biscany in St Elizabeth Parish, Canmoreock in Hanover Parish and Glasgow in Westmoreland Parish.[465] He was also married to the daughter of Robert Colhoun (or Colquhoun) of St Kitts and his grandfather was William Cunninghame of Craigends estate. His other properties included Cessnock in Ayrshire, Neilstonside in Renfrewshire, and Whitehill House, Glasgow, which he bought from John Glassford in 1759. John's brother, Hugh (d. 1774), spent time in Jamaica and, apart from being a joint owner of Biscany, was also an owner of Aberdeen, Craigie and Eldersley estates, all in St Elizabeth Parish. John's estates passed to his son Robert[466] (1773-1855), who had to sell Kelly in 1846 due to the loss in value of the Jamaican properties. He retired to Seafield Cottage, Greenock. Before this downturn in fortunes, however, Robert and his brother, the soldier Sir

The 1890 Kelly House after the fire on 5 December 1913. The blaze was blamed on Suffragists, who had burned several large houses across the UK mostly belonging to polititians opposed to women's suffrage. It was reported that Suffragette literature was found at the scene. However, the house had lain empty, awaiting sale, for six months, raising the possibility that there was an electrical fire which began unnoticed in the empty property and the ongoing militant campaign of the Suffrage Movement provided an excuse to cover the neglect.

James Maxwell Wallace (1785-1867; settled in Yorkshire), shared in awards of over £15,348 from the Slave Compensation Commission; 757 people were enslaved in the estates they profited from. Kelly estate was later owned by the chemist and anti-slavery campaigner James 'Paraffin' Young[467] (1811-83). Kelly House was subsequently demolished and rebuilt in 1890. The second house was burned down in 1913[468] and the site of the estate is now taken by a caravan holiday park.

Slavery voyages from Greenock and Port Glasgow

In the 350 years of the slave trade it is estimated that over 12 million people were taken from Africa and forced into slavery. Of these around 1.8 million died en route.
Shipping for the British slave trade was mainly based in English ports such as Liverpool, London and Bristol. Nonetheless, Scottish ports played a part: 27 slave ships left Scotland in the eighteenth century, 19 of them from Greenock and Port Glasgow.[469] All of these ships journeyed from Scotland to West Africa, carrying goods which were traded for people, who were then taken to be sold at locations including Virginia, Barbados, Grenada, St Kitts, Martinique and Brazil.
There were eleven voyages by slave ships from Greenock between 1759 and 1766, delivering 1,836 people who survived the journey into slavery. From Port Glasgow there were five voyages between 1717 and 1762, with 654 African people disembarking at their destinations.[470]

REFERENCES

351. 'William Cunninghame 14th of Craigends', *LBS database*: https://www.ucl.ac.uk/lbs/person/view/2146631123
352. Stuart Nisbet, 'Renfrewshire's Slave Legacy 3: The Cunninghams of Craigends', 2019, *Renfrewshire Local History Forum*: https://rlhf.info/renfrewshires-slave-legacy-3-the-cunninghams-of-craigends/
353. 'Dunstaffnage [Jamaica | Westmoreland', *LBS database*: http://wwwdepts-live.ucl.ac.uk/lbs/estate/view/6442
354. 'Craigends House', *Canmore*: https://canmore.org.uk/site/142878/houston-craigends-house
355. 'Robert Cunninghame Cunninghame Graham', *LBS database*: http://wwwdepts-live.ucl.ac.uk/lbs/person/view/2146634582
356. 'Archibald Campbell of Inverawe', *LBS database*: https://www.ucl.ac.uk/lbs/person/view/2146660319
357. Dairmid Campbell, 'A Brief Overview of the Descent of Inverawe', *The Campbells of Inverawe*: http://www.inverawe.org.uk/a-brief-overview-of-the-descent-of-inverawe/
358. Dairmid Campbell, *A History of the MacConnochie Campbells of Inverawe*, Vol. III, 2014, p. 64: http://www.inverawe.org.uk/publications/MacConnochie-Campbells-VolumeThree-Diarmid-Campbell.pdf
359. *Inverclyde*, pp. 27-32.
360. ''Racist' Gourock Coat of Arms set to be replaced', 21.1.2022, *Greenock Telegraph*: https://www.greenocktelegraph.co.uk/news/19858545.racist-gourock-coat-arms-set-replaced/
361. *Inverclyde*, p. 39.
362. 'Grand Style of Gourock House', 6.3.2014, *Greenock Telegraph*: https://www.greenocktelegraph.co.uk/opinion/14014067.grand-style-of-gourock-house/
363. David Alston, 'George Rainy's wives', *Slaves and Highlanders*: https://www.spanglefish.com/slavesandhighlanders/index.asp?pageid=604812
364. *Inverclyde*, p. 39.
365. 'Archibald Graham Lang', *LBS database*: https://www.ucl.ac.uk/lbs/person/view/46924
366. 'Gray, Roxburgh & Co.', *LBS database*: https://www.ucl.ac.uk/lbs/firm/view/1285529841
367. Thomas Nugent, 'Site of Kempock House', 2011, *Geograph*: https://www.geograph.org.uk/photo/2463437
368. *Inverclyde*, pps. 19, 39, 41, 42.
369. Dwayne Wong (Omowale), 'From Slavery to Dictatorship: A Brief History of Togo's Struggle', *Huffington Post*, 13.11.2017: https://www.huffpost.com/entry/from-slavery-to-dictatorship-a-brief-history-of-togos_b_5a049f07e4b0204d0c17153f#:~:text=Togo%20was%20one%20of%20the,were%20taken%20from%20that%20region
370. James Hunter, 'Many of Greenock's streets were left nameless until 1775', *Greenock Telegraph*, 10.2.2015: https://www.greenocktelegraph.co.uk/opinion/14018780.many-of-greenockrsquos-streets-were-left-nameless-until-1775/
371. McLean Museum and Art Gallery, 'Sugar', 2022, *Inverclyde Council*: https://www.inverclyde.gov.uk/community-life-and-leisure/heritage-services/collections/watt-library/local-history/sugar
372. *Inverclyde*, p. 41.
373. Sheryllynne Haggerty and Susanne Seymour, 'Imperial careering and enslavement in the long eighteenth century: the Bentinck family, 1710–1830s', p. 10, University of Nottingham, 2018.
374. '*Zong* massacre', *Wikipedia*: https://en.wikipedia.org/wiki/Zong_massacre
375. McLean Museum and Art Gallery, 'Sugar', 2022, *Inverclyde Council*: https://www.inverclyde.gov.uk/community-life-and-leisure/heritage-services/collections/watt-library/local-history/sugar
376. Robert Murray Smith, *The History of Greenock*, 1921, p. 101: https://www.inverclyde.gov.uk/assets/attach/5139/R.M.-Smith-The-History-of-Greenock-Complete-CC.pdf
377. 'Agnew Crawford', *LBS database*: https://www.ucl.ac.uk/lbs/person/view/1339661395
378. 'Robin's Hall', *LBS database*: https://www.ucl.ac.uk/lbs/estate/view/2739
379. *Inverclyde*, p. 44.
380. McLean Museum and Art Gallery, 'Sugar', 2022, *Inverclyde Council*: https://www.inverclyde.gov.uk/community-life-and-leisure/heritage-services/collections/watt-library/local-history/sugar
381. 'Customs House, Greenock', *Scottish Civic Trust MyPlace*: https://myplacescotland.org.uk/awards_entry/custom-house-greenock/
382. 'Greenock Customs House', 7.8.2015, *The Greenockian*: http://thegreenockian.blogspot.com/2015/08/greenock-custom-house.html
383. *Inverclyde*, p. 44.
384. Ibid., p. 40.
385. Ibid., p. 43.
386. J. Ferran, 'Marion Fairrie', 2019, *Ohanov, Fiechter, Ferran, Persohn & Co.*: https://www.monchique.com/Ochanoff/ohanov/ochanoff/6895.htm
387. *Inverclyde*, pp. 36-37.
388. *Glasgow, Slavery and Atlantic Commerce*, p. 102.
389. Dr S. Mullen and Prof. S Newman, *Slavery, abolition and the University of Glasgow: report and recommendations of the University of Glasgow History of Slavery Steering Committee*, 2018, quoted in *Inverclyde*, p. 35.
390. Stephen Mullen, 'James Watt and Slavery in Scotland', 17.8.2020, *History Workshop*: https://www.historyworkshop.org.uk/anti-racism/james-watt-and-slavery-in-scotland/#:~:text=Overall%2C%20the%20Watt%20enterprise%20involved,illegal%20in%20Scotland%20in%201778.

391. 'John Mcfarquhar', *LBS database*, http://wwwdepts-live.ucl.ac.uk/lbs/person/view/2146630945
392. *Inverclyde*, p. 53.
393. McLean Museum and Art Gallery, 'Sugar', 2022, *Inverclyde Council*: https://www.inverclyde.gov.uk/community-life-and-leisure/heritage-services/collections/watt-library/local-history/sugar
394. *Inverclyde*, p. 44.
395. Ibid., p. 40.
396. 'Sir Michael Shaw Stewart, 5th Baronet', *Wikipedia*: https://en.wikipedia.org/wiki/Sir_Michael_Shaw_Stewart,_5th_Baronet
397. *Inverclyde*, p. 47.
398. 'Robert Wallace', *LBS database*: https://www.ucl.ac.uk/lbs/person/view/19150
399. Lairich Rig, 'Memorial to Robert Wallace', *Geograph*: https://www.geograph.org.uk/photo/2623837
400. McLean Museum and Art Gallery, 'Sugar', 2022, *Inverclyde Council*: https://www.inverclyde.gov.uk/community-life-and-leisure/heritage-services/collections/watt-library/local-history/sugar
401. *Inverclyde*, p. 44.
402. McLean Museum and Art Gallery, 'Sugar', 2022, *Inverclyde Council*: https://www.inverclyde.gov.uk/community-life-and-leisure/heritage-services/collections/watt-library/local-history/sugar
403. 'James Tasker', *LBS database*: https://www.ucl.ac.uk/lbs/person/view/43765
404. *Inverclyde*, p. 44.
405. Ibid., p. 41.
406. Ibid., p. 49.
407. 'Greenock, Mansion House', *Canmore*: https://canmore.org.uk/site/41301/greenock-mansion-house
408. 'Elizabeth Martin', *LBS database*: https://www.ucl.ac.uk/lbs/person/view/14717 / 'John Martin of Greenock', *LBS database*: https://www.ucl.ac.uk/lbs/person/view/2146651939
409. 'Arthur Oughterson Senior', *LBS database*: https://www.ucl.ac.uk/lbs/person/view/2146648573
410. 'Barbados 3661 (Brighton)', *LBS database*: https://www.ucl.ac.uk/lbs/claim/view/3587
411. 'Dugald Malcolm Ruthven', *LBS database*: https://www.ucl.ac.uk/lbs/person/view/2146661223
412. 'Unknown', *LBS database*:: https://www.ucl.ac.uk/lbs/estate/view/17581
413. 'The History of George Dale, a native of Africa, 1790', National Records of Scotland: https://www.nrscotland.gov.uk/research/learning/slavery/the-history-of-george-dale-a-native-of-africa-1790
414. Alison Campsie, 'How Scots fishing towns boomed from sale of salted herring to slave plantations', 9.8.2020, *The Scotsman*: https://www.scotsman.com/heritage-and-retro/heritage/how-scots-fishing-towns-boomed-sale-salted-herring-slave-plantations-2936978
415. 'Sir James Campbell of Houstoun', *LBS database*: https://www.ucl.ac.uk/lbs/person/view/2146650411
416. Stuart Nisbet, 'The Old Village of Houston', 2015, *Renfrewshire Local History Forum*: https://rlhf.info/the-old-village-of-houston/
417. 'William Maxwell Alexander', *LBS database*: https://www.ucl.ac.uk/lbs/person/view/40802
418. Nicholas Kingsley, '(85) Alexander (later Hagart-Alexander) of Ballochmyle, baronets', 2013, *Landed Families of Britain and Ireland*: https://landedfamilies.blogspot.com/2013/10/85-alexander-later-hagart-alexander-of.html
419. 'Sir John Shaw Steart 4th Bart.', *LBS database*: https://www.ucl.ac.uk/lbs/person/view/2146651959
420. 'Archibald Stewart of Tobago', *LBS database*: https://www.ucl.ac.uk/lbs/person/view/2146632274
421. 'Houston Stewart', *LBS database*: https://www.ucl.ac.uk/lbs/person/view/27793
422. 'Sir Michael Shaw Stewart 6th Bart.', *LBS database*: https://www.ucl.ac.uk/lbs/person/view/2146636353
423. 'James Milliken I', *LBS database*: https://www.ucl.ac.uk/lbs/person/view/2146645491
424. 'Milliken House', *Canmore*: https://canmore.org.uk/site/43226/milliken-house
425. 'James Milliken I', *LBS database*.
426. Stuart Nisbet, 'Renfrewshire's Slave Legacy 2: The Napiers of Milliken', 2019, *Renfrewshire Local History Forum*: https://rlhf.info/renfrewshires-slave-legacy-2-the-napiers-of-milliken/
427. 'James Milliken II', 'James Milliken I', *LBS database*: https://www.ucl.ac.uk/lbs/person/view/2146647687
428. Stuart Nisbet, 'Renfrewshire's Slave Legacy 2: The Napiers of Milliken', 2019, *Renfrewshire Local History Forum*.
429. 'Alexander Porterfield of Porterfield', *LBS database*: https://www.ucl.ac.uk/lbs/person/view/2146650419 and 'Boyd Porterfield of Duchal', *LBS database*: https://www.ucl.ac.uk/lbs/person/view/2146650419
430. 'Alexander Ferrier of Surinam', *LBS database*: https://www.ucl.ac.uk/lbs/person/view/2146646371
431. 'Celia Scott (nee King)', *LBS database*: https://www.ucl.ac.uk/lbs/person/view/46768
432. 'Daniel King of Tobago', *LBS database*: https://www.ucl.ac.uk/lbs/person/view/2146638985

433. 'Tobago 12 (Sherwood Park)', *LBS database*: https://www.ucl.ac.uk/lbs/claim/view/27819
434. 'Col. William McDowall I', *LBS database*: https://www.ucl.ac.uk/lbs/person/view/2146646095
435. Stuart Nisbet, 'The Harveys of Castle Semple: Part 1: The Early Years (c. 1700-1815)', 2013, *Renfrewshire Local History Journal* Vol. 17: https://rlhf.info/wp-content/uploads/17.3.1%20Castle%20Semple%20Nisbet.pdf
436. 'William McDowall II', *LBS database*: https://www.ucl.ac.uk/lbs/person/view/2146646097
437. 'William McDowall of Garthland and Castle Semple', *The Univerisity of Glasgow Story*: https://universitystory.gla.ac.uk/biography/?id=WH1163&type=P and 'William McDowall III of Garthland', *LBS database*: https://www.ucl.ac.uk/lbs/person/view/2146640675
438. 'William McDowall the younger of Castle Semple', *LBS database*: https://www.ucl.ac.uk/lbs/person/view/10609
439. 'Margaret Harvey', *LBS database*: https://www.ucl.ac.uk/lbs/person/view/42078
440. Elizabeth West, 'The Harveys of Castle Semple Part 2: The Later Years (c. 1815-1908)', 2013, *Renfrewshire Local History Forum* Journal Vol. 17: http://rlhf.info/wp-content/uploads/17.3.2%20Castle%20Semple%20West.pdf
441. John Wallace (1715 – abt. 1807), *WikiTree*: https://www.wikitree.com/wiki/Wallace-7788
442. 'Blackhall Manor', Paisley.org.uk: https://www.paisley.org.uk/paisley-history/blackhall-manor/
443. 'Ralston', *Old Country Houses*: http://www.glasgowwestaddress.co.uk/Old_Country_Houses/Ralston.htm
444. *Inverclyde*, p. 44.
445. Ibid., p. 41.
446. 'Peter Montgomerie', *LBS database*: https://www.ucl.ac.uk/lbs/person/view/28688
447. 'Robert Montgomerie', *LBS database*: https://www.ucl.ac.uk/lbs/person/view/2146631274
448. 'Sevilla Estate', *LBS database*: https://www.ucl.ac.uk/lbs/estate/view/3806
449. 'Robert Farquhar', *LBS database*: https://www.ucl.ac.uk/lbs/person/view/11426
450. Andy Sweet, 'Newark Castle', 2003-23, *Stravaiging Around Scotland*: http://www.stravaiging.com/history/castle/newark-castle/
451. Stuart Nisbet, 'Uncovering the History of Greenbank', 2010, *Mearns Local History Group*: https://www.mearnshistory.org.uk/index.php/history/mansion-houses/history-of-greenbank
452. The Watt Institution, *The Gourock Ropework Company*: https://www.inverclyde.gov.uk/assets/attach/14408/the-gourock-ropework-company.pdf
453. 'Port Glasgow Rope and Duck Company', 12.1.2021, *The Greenockian*: http://thegreenockian.blogspot.com/2021/01/port-glasgow-rope-and-duck-company.html
454. *Inverclyde*, p. 49.
455. 'Alexander Fairley Harrower', *LBS database*: https://www.ucl.ac.uk/lbs/person/view/7379
456. 'Jamie Montgomery, Runaway Slave', 14.8.2018, *Legacies of Slavery*: https://glasgowmuseumsslavery.co.uk/2018/08/14/jamie-montgomery-runaway-slave/
457. 'Eldersie House', *Canmore*: https://canmore.org.uk/site/44202/eldersie-house
458. 'History', *Eldersie Estates*: http://www.eldersie.org/history.html https://blogs.ed.ac.uk/managingimperiallegacies/sites/vitruvius-britannicus/
459. George Manzor, 'Alexander Speirs – Tobacco Lord (1714 – 1782) Part 1', 2020, *Glasgow's Benefactors*: https://glasgowbenefactors.com/2020/03/14/alexander-speirs-tobacco-lord-1714-1785-part-1/comment-page-1/#_ednref11
460. Ibid.
461. 'Eldersie House', *Canmore*.
462. 'Blythswood House', *TheGlasgowStory*: https://www.theglasgowstory.com/image/?inum=TGSB00240&t=2
463. Ibid.
464. *Glasgow, Slavery and Atlantic Commerce*, p. 61.
465. 'John Wallace of Cessnock and Kelly', *LBS database*: https://www.ucl.ac.uk/lbs/person/view/2146639039
466. 'Robert Wallace', *LBS database*: https://www.ucl.ac.uk/lbs/person/view/19150
467. 'RSC honours forgotten Scottish scientific hero', 9.11.2011, *Royal Society of Chemistry*: https://www.rsc.org/news-events/articles/2011/11-november/rsc-honours-forgotten-scottish-scientific-hero/
468. 'Wemyss Bay, Kelly House', *Canmore*: https://canmore.org.uk/site/40694/wemyss-bay-kelly-house
469. 'Glasgow and the slave trade', *It Wisnae Us*: https://it.wisnae.us/glasgow-and-the-slave-trade/#:~:text=The%20first%20slave%20voyage%20from,the%20West%20Indies%20and%20Virginia.
470. 'Trans-Atlantic Slave Trade – Database', *Slave Voyages*: https://www.slavevoyages.org/voyage/database

The north bank of the Clyde estuary: Clydebank to Dunoon

Alexandria

Tulliechewan

This area of Alexandria is named after the castle that once stood in grounds on the west side of the A82, opposite today's Woodbank Gardens. This was the home of Glasgow merchant William Campbell who had trading links to the Caribbean. The castle, built around 1808, was demolished in 1954.[472]

Tullichewan Castle.

Clydebank

Mountblow Road

The estate of Mountblow from 1767[473] belonged to Robert Donald (1724-1803). From about 1735 he was in business in Glasgow as a tobacco merchant, becoming a tobacco lord and serving twice as Lord Provost of the city.[474] He built Mountblow House on purchasing the estate and remained in it even after he was made bankrupt twenty years later as he was employed by the city to oversee works to deepen the River Clyde.[475] In 1793 he had occasion to write to George Washington to remind him that they had met in the early 1750s at the residence of Robert Dinwiddie, Governor of Virginia (see *Glasgow: Germiston*).[476]

Dumbarton

Denny Shipbuilders

The shipyard of William Denny & Sons was based just below the rock where the River Leven flows into the Clyde. Between 1844 and its closure in 1963 it built over 1,500 ships.[477] During the American Civil War of 1861-65, Denny built twenty ships for the Confederate states to be used as blockade-runners, warships and privateers.[478] These ships contributed to the survival of the Confederate slavery-based economy, as they were used for the export of goods such as plantation-produced cotton (often to British cotton manufacturers) and to bring in supplies. Denny produced eight known blockade runners but were not alone in this business among Clyde shipbuilders: Lumsden of Arden, Scott & Co. of Greenock, William Simons & Co. of Renfrew, Alexander Stephen & Sons of Glasgow, J. & G. Thomson / John Brown & Co. of Clydebank and Tod & McGregor of Glasgow all built blockade-runners for the Confederacy.[479] Tod & McGregor was the launch-place of the ship *Dolphin* in Jules Verne's novella *Les Forceurs de blocus* (*The Blockade Runners*), an adventure story about a blockade-runner.

Denny's Shipyard from Dumbarton Rock, 1911.

Dunoon

Castle House

This was built in 1822 as his 'marine villa'[480] by Caribbean plantation owner James Ewing (1775-1853). It was sold to Dunoon Town Council in 1893 and became the Castle House Museum in 1998.

Cardross

Camis Eskan House, Colgrain Estate

East of Cardross lies Camis Eskin House on the estate of Colgrain. The estate was owned by the Dennistoun family from 1351 and the house dates from 1648[481] though it has been extended and redeveloped over the centuries.

James Dennistoun of Colgrain (1731-96) inherited the estate in 1752, by which time he had decided to 'devote himself to the peaceful pursuits of commerce'; in 1746 he had taken an oath of loyalty to the government, having been prevented by his father from joining Charles Edward Stuart's Jacobite Rebellion the previous

Camis Easkin House.

year.[482] He went on to establish the Caribbean firm of Dennistoun, Buchanan and his sons Richard and Robert followed him into the trade. James's grandson, also James (d. 1834), was in turn a partner in the firm and also of William Duff & Co. of New Providence, Bahamas, which – according to the *Bahamas Slave Register 1822* – enslaved nine people in 1822. The company also operated in Jamaica.[483]

Caribbean and Demerara merchant Colin Campbell (1782-1863) bought Colgrain[484] in 1836. He was the son of John Campbell who set up Caribbean merchants John Campbell Senior & Co. On his death he left the stupendous sum of £169,351, some of which came from compensation for the loss of 2,093 people who were enslaved on eleven estates he and his firm were connected to – nine in Demerara (now part of Guyana), one in Grenada and one in St Vincent. The compensation amounted to over £87,913 and was shared between Campbell and his business partners, who included a number of Campbell relatives.[485] Campbell's son, also Colin (d. 1886), continued in the Demerara sugar production industry and died worth £627,000. The firm became Curtis Campbell, later merging with Booker McConnell.

Colin Campbell had the house remodelled in 1840 (further alterations were carried out in subsequent decades)[486] and it and the estate remained in the Campbell family until it was sold to Dunbartonshire County Council in 1946.[487] For a time it was used as a hospital, then converted into flats in 1979.

Cardross Park Mansions

Cardross Park House.

The house of Cardross Park, off Braid Drive, was owned by Banffshire-born Charles Edmonstone (1757-1827) after his return from a career as a plantation owner in Demerara (now part of Guyana). He was there from 1780 to 1817, establishing the timber-cutting estate at Mibiri Creek on the Demerara River. There he married Helen Reid, the daughter of a fellow Banffshire man whose own wife was the daughter of an Arawak chief. Edmonstone became celebrated locally for his skills – assisted by Arawak tribesmen – in hunting down runaway slaves.[488] When he left the country, the 'Inhabitants of Demerary' thanked him for his '... command of repeated expeditions, against the revolted negroes of Guiana ... his courage, always ensured success'.[489] His business in Demerara continued after he left: 87 people enslaved on his estate were registered for him in 1826. After his death the following year, his will allowed for the freeing of three of these people, all female.[490]

Edmonstone's daughter Anne married the English naturalist and Demerara plantation manager Charles Waterton (1782-1865), who on his return to Britain brought back John Edmonston, an enslaved man who had been freed by Waterton and whom he taught taxidermy of birds. John Edmonston then taught Charles Darwin this skill.[491]

Charles Edmonstone's nephew, Archibald Edmonstone (1786-1856), was also in Demerara, registering 122 enslaved people engaged in 'wood cutting'. He was the beneficiary of compensation awards of over £6,797 for 128 people enslaved on two Demerara estates, one of which was called Waratilla Creek.[492]

Cardross Park has since been converted into apartments.

Carman Road

Off Carman Road lies Bloomhill House, built around 1838 by plantation owner Alexander Ferrier (1789-1848). Previous to building the house he resided at

Bloomhill House.

The unoccupied Bloomhill House, 2023.

Springbank, Kilmalcolm, likely to have been his home on his return from Surinam (now Suriname) where he jointly owned two plantations in the Commewijne district, Alkmaar and Frederickdorp. Suriname was a major producer of sugar and a Dutch colony. (While the Netherlands' transatlantic slave trade ended in 1814, slavery in its colonies was maintained until 1863, though many former slaves remained at work on plantations until 1873 so that owners were buffered from financial loss.[493])

Despite his return to Scotland, Ferrier continued his activities in Suriname. In 1844 Alkmaar alone enslaved around 600 people, transported from Africa by Ferrier and his business partner, Thomas Butler Parry of London. At that time, both were described by a British consul as men 'long notoriously and successfully engaged in this unhallowed traffic in human flesh.'[494] This consul, Edward W. H. Schenley, wrote despatches to the Earl of Aberdeen, Foreign Secretary 1841-46, reporting on the plantation system of Surinam and the barbaric treatment of enslaved people, including shootings, whippings and torture, details of which were reported to the Dutch government by the British.[495]

Ferrier's daughter, Margaret Gourlay Ferrier (1832-1900), inherited his shares in these plantations and was named in an 1860 Parliamentary report into British people still profiting from slavery. The report noted that in 1852, when the Netherlands government was considering a Bill that would have freed the children of enslaved people on birth, Margaret Ferrier was among plantation owners who petitioned the British Ambassador to The Hague to 'use his influence . . . to obtain compensation for them, and for the yet unborn children of the slave mothers they owned . . .'[496] By the time Dutch slavery was abolished Alkmaar was enslaving 445 people.[497]

Meanwhile, in 1858[498] Margaret had married the artist Joseph Noel Paton (1821-1901), later appointed 'H.M. Limner for Scotland' (i.e the Queen's miniature-portrait painter) in 1865. They settled at No. 33 George Square, Edinburgh[499], and she is the subject of his 1862 painting 'The Lullaby', which is now on display at the Scottish National Portrait Gallery in a display entitled 'Heroes and Heroines: Idealism and Achievement in the Victorian Age'. In 1862/63, Margaret Ferrier and her children were compensated by the Dutch government for their ownership share of the enslaved people at Alkmaar.[500] The historian David Alston notes that she 'was one of the last slave-owners in Scotland.'[501] She and her husband are buried at Dean Cemetery, Edinburgh.

Bloomhill House was most recently a care home for the elderly, which was shut down after concerns were raised about the way it was being run. Approval was then given for the building to be converted to apartments though at the time of writing it remains unoccupied.

Geilston

Geilston House, north-west of Cardross, was built for Glasgow tobacco merchant James Donald (1713-60).[502] The estate, house and business was inherited by his son Thomas (1744-98), who married Janet Dunlop, daughter of another tobacco lord, Colin Dunlop.[503] The Donald family sold Geilston in 1805. Thomas Dunlop's son, Colin Dunlop Donald (1777-1859), became a lawyer (described as a 'Tory of the Tories' who preferred candles to newfangled gas lighting)[504] and in this capacity, acting as an executor, was able to share in the award of over £1,889 paid out in 1836 for the 89 people enslaved at Hermitage estates, St David Parish, Jamaica. Geilston House still stands; its garden is open to the public, maintained by the National Trust for Scotland.

Geilston House.

Renton

Strathleven House

Completed in 1708, this house was purchased by Glasgow merchant James Ewing (1772-1853) in 1830; he was Lord Provost of Glasgow in 1832/33 and also MP for the city from 1832 to 1835. A fellow of the Royal Society of Edinburgh, he also received an honorary degree from Glasgow University. With partner William Mathieson, in 1803 he created the Caribbean trading firm James Ewing & Co. and in 1807 he helped to establish the pro-slavery lobbying group, the Glasgow West India Association. He was a Dean of Guild of the Merchants House and owned plantations in Jamaica which, combined, enslaved 586 people; the Slave Compensation Commission awarded him over £9,327 on abolition.[505] After his death, his wife Jane continued to live at Strathleven until her death in 1896. Thereafter it was inherited by another family. It fell into some disrepair but was fully restored and is now a conference and wedding venue.[506] Ewing also lived in Crawford Mansion, Queen Street, Glasgow and built Castle House, Dunoon.

Strathleven House.

REFERENCES

472. 'Tulliechewan Castle', *West Dunbartonshire Council*: https://www.west-dunbarton.gov.uk/leisure-parks-events/museums-and-galleries/collections/buildings/castles-and-country-houses/castles-and-country-houses-vale-of-leven/tullichewan-castle/
473. 'Mountblow', *Old Country Houses*: http://www.glasgowwestaddress.co.uk/Old_Country_Houses/Mountblow.htm
474. *Glasgow, Slavery and Atlantic Commerce*, p. 77.
475. 'Mountblow House', *TheGlasgowStory*: https://www.theglasgowstory.com/image/?inum=TGSB00303
476. 'To George Washington from Robert Donald, 6 June 1793', *Founders Online*: https://founders.archives.gov/documents/Washington/05-13-02-0022
477. 'Denny's Shipyard', *Clyde Waterfront*: http://www.clydewaterfront.com/clyde-heritage/dumbarton/denny's-shipyard#:~:text=Denny's%2C%20the%20most%20famous%20Dumbarton,first%20turbine%20steamer%20in%201901.
478. 'October 2013 Meeting – The Blockade Runners', *Clyde River Steamer Club*: https://crsc.org.uk/archive/previous-meetings/oct2013meeting/#:~:text=Denny%20built%2020%20blockade%2Drunners,from%20the%20company's%20official%20history).
479. 'Blockade running during the American Civil War: Sources', 2011, *University of Glasgow Archive Services*: https://www.gla.ac.uk/media/Media_60666_smxx.pdf
480. 'Castle House, Castle Gardens', *Historic Environment Scotland*: http://portal.historicenvironment.scot/designation/LB26434
481. 'Camis Eskan House', *Canmore*: https://canmore.org.uk/site/42513/camis-eskan-house
482. 'Some Account of the Family of Dennistoun of Colgrain', 1859, p. 20; 'Histories of Scottish Families', *National Library of Scotland*: https://digital.nls.uk/histories-of-scottish-families/archive/95535117#?c=0&m=0&s=0&cv=0&xywh=-1247%2C-186%2C4992%2C3701
483. 'James Dennistoun of Dennistoun', *LBS database*: http://wwwdepts-live.ucl.ac.uk/lbs/person/view/2146642451
484. Stephen Mullen, 'The Great Glasgow West India House of John Campbell, Senior, & Co.', *Recovering Scotland's Slavery Past – The Caribbean Connection*, ed. T.M. Devine, Edinburgh University Press, 2015, p. 139.
485. 'Colin Campbell of Colgrain', *LBS database*: http://wwwdepts-live.ucl.ac.uk/lbs/person/view/6745
486. 'M002 Camis Eskan, Craigendoran', 2014, *Mackintosh Architecture – Context, Making and Meaning, University of Glasgow*: https://www.mackintosh-architecture.gla.ac.uk/catalogue/pdf/M002.pdf
487. Donald Fullarton, 'The Campbells of Camis Eskan', 8.10.2014, *Helensburgh Heritage Trust*: http://www.helensburgh-heritage.co.uk/index.php?option=com_content&view=article&id=1182:the-campbells-of-camis-eskan&catid=39:people-&Itemid=399#:~:text=It%20was%20built%20by%20the,to%20Colin%20Campbell%20from%20Renfrewshire.
488. David Alston, 'Charles Edmonstone', *Slaves & Highlanders*.: https://www.spanglefish.com/slavesandhighlanders/index.asp?pageid=222592
489. Ibid.
490. 'Charles Edmonstone', *LBS database*: http://wwwdepts-live.ucl.ac.uk/lbs/person/view/2146638175
491. 'Charles Waterton', *LBS database*: http://wwwdepts-live.ucl.ac.uk/lbs/person/view/2146630589
492. 'Archibald Edmonstone', *LBS database*: http://wwwdepts-live.ucl.ac.uk/lbs/person/view/8606
493. 'Slavery Memorial Year 1 July 2023 to 1 July 2024', *Ministry of Education, Culture and Science, Government of the Netherlands*: https://www.government.nl/ministries/ministry-of-education-culture-and-science/events/slavery-memorial-year#:~:text=On%201%20July%201863%2C%20slavery,the%20Kingdom%20of%20the%20Netherlands.
494. David Alston, 'Alexander Ferrier (Cardross)', *Slaves & Highlanders*.: https://www.spanglefish.com/slavesandhighlanders/index.asp?pageid=608092
495. *General Report of the Colonial Land and Emigration Commissioners*, Vol. 2, H.M. Stationery Office, 1845: https://books.google.co.uk/books?id=JZItAQAAMAAJ&printsec=frontcover#v=onepage&q&f=false
496. *Accounts and Papers: Slave Trade, Session 24 January – 28 August 1860, Vol. LXX*, (Paliamentary Papers Vol. 70), H.M. Stationery Office, 1860, p. 75: https://books.google.co.uk/books?id=N9kSAAAAYAAJ&dq=%22alexander%20ferrier%22%20surinam&pg=RA1-PA80#v=snippet&q=Ferrier&f=false
497. 'Plantation Alkmaar. Alkmaar in Suriname, 1745-present', Oneindig Noord-Holland: https://onh.nl/nieuws/plantage-alkmaar-in-suriname
498. Emily Learmont, 'Childhood enshrined: *The Lullaby* (1862) by Joseph Noel Paton (1821-1901), *The British Art Journal*, Vol. 20, No. 1 (Spring/Summer 2019), p. 30.

499. Ibid.
500. 'Alexander Ferrier of Surinam', *LBS database*: http://wwwdepts-live.ucl.ac.uk/lbs/person/view/2146646371
501. David Alston, 'Alexander Ferrier (Cardross)', *Slaves & Highlanders*.
502. 'Thomas Donald', *We Relate*: https://www.werelate.org/wiki/Person:Thomas_Donald_(2)
503. Ibid.
504. 'Colin Dunlop Donald', *LBS database*: http://wwwdepts-live.ucl.ac.uk/lbs/person/view/42997 – the quote comes from the entry on Donald from James MacLehose, *Memoirs and portraits of one hundred Glasgow men who have died during the last thirty years and in their lives did much to make the city what it now is*, 1886.
505. *Glasgow, Slavery and Atlantic Commerce*, p. 81.
506. 'Strathleven House', *Scottish Historic Buildings Trust*: https://www.shbt.org.uk/our-buildings/strathleven-house/